BORDER CROSSING

BORDER CROSSING

A Spiritual Journey

KATIE FUNK WIEBE

HERALD PRESS
Scottdale, Pennsylvania
Waterloo, Ontario

Library of Congress Cataloging-in-Publication Data
Wiebe, Katie Funk.
 Border crossing : a spiritual journey / Katie Funk Wiebe.
  p. cm.
 ISBN 0-8361-9013-0 (alk. paper)
  1. Aging—Religious aspects—Christianity. 2. Aged women—
Religious life. 3. Christian life—Mennonite authors. I. Title.
BV4580.W47 1995
248.8'5—dc20   94-23616
                                                  CIP

All Bible quotations are used by permission, all rights reserved, and
unless otherwise indicated are from *The Holy Bible, New International
Version*, copyright © 1973, 1978, 1984 International Bible Society,
Zondervan Bible Publishers.

BORDER CROSSING
Copyright © 1995 by Herald Press, Scottdale, Pa. 15683
     Published simultaneously in Canada by Herald Press,
     Waterloo, Ont. N2L 6H7. All rights reserved
Library of Congress Catalog Number: 94-23616
International Standard Book Number: 0-8361-9013-0
Printed in the United States of America
Cover art and book design by Gwen M. Stamm

00 99 98 97 96 95 10 9 8 7 6 5 4 3 2 1

To my children: Joanna, Susan, Christine, James

Contents

A big thank you to the older adults in my circle of friends who inspired me, and to my daughter Christine who kept me working at this manuscript when I wanted to quit—and for her careful suggestions.

Preface

I thought I had planned well for retirement, what I was going to do, where I was going to live, what I was going to live on, and who I wanted to be close to.

Therefore I was surprised when I found myself going through a low-grade depression, in dissonance with myself but also with the world at large. Thirty years earlier, when I became a widow, I had gone through a severe identity crisis. I found extremely difficult the transition from being a member of a couple to being alone in a society that at that time did not make much room for single parents.

Was my present frustration a repeat of that but under different circumstances? Could I, by openly writing about it, dignify the discomfort which I was feeling and which I sensed others in the same circumstances were feeling? Could I turn this border crossing into an account that might be meaningful to others?

I probed my ambivalences about this life stage. The probing started a backward look to my growing up, to the aging of my parents and friends. I thought about other life stages and the securities and satisfactions of each.

This book is a record of that probing and my experience in crossing the border into the land of aging. During this time one feels the uneasiness of being between non-identity and joyous self-confidence. The boundary of this land of aging is undefined, yet entering this stage is a border crossing, nevertheless.

I know all retirees do not have my experience. But I believe that people who have found much satisfaction in their careers may find the road slippery when they begin to cross over. Men, more so than women, have difficulty with retirement from work that provided them with their main identity in life. In the future, women will experience this transition more directly. Some men and women glide across without a hitch, of course. But I didn't. And that is why I write.

I hoped to write frankly. The process of growing older forces admission of human imperfection and mortality. Life is going to end. We older adults are part of a vulnerable group, yet a powerful one. We have wisdom, experience, money, and loyalty.

Yet what does accumulated experience count for? I recognize that I am probably a better teacher now when I am not teaching than when I began thirty years ago, but I am not now teaching. Nor are many other older adults who have years of experience in their fields now active in them. What is this accumulated wisdom for? To rot?

These memoirs and reflections confess my valleys and my mountains. I wanted this writing to be inspirational rather than informational. Therefore I leave the topics of medical care, housing, and financial and legal arrangements to the experts. Instead I have added many stories, knowing a story has the greatest form of power to clarify, to name and rename. In addition to my own journey, I discuss such matters as older adult spirituality, servanthood, creativity, humor, life review, and facing change.

As I wrote and rewrote, the main question hammering itself into my consciousness during these border-crossing years was what God has in mind for the older adult—and especially for me. Where do those in the last quarter or third of life fit into God's overall plan?

Some six to eight months into the project, it became clear to me that what I was trying to do was develop a theology of aging. I had already done a biblical study of aging (*Life After Fifty: A Positive Look at Aging in the Faith Community*, Faith & Life). Now I wanted to take this one step further and in a different direction.

Theologian Krister Stendall writes that "theology is worrying about what God worries about when God gets up in the morning: the mending of creation." What does God worry about regarding older adults? Some ministries to the older adult contribute to feelings of despair, futility, and loneliness because they are not tied to life purposes. Activity is encouraged for the sake of activity, which soon increases a sense of uselessness. Disengagement from life and waiting for death is not good for mental health. When people become older, what needs mending in their relationship to God and humanity? That is the essence of this book.

I recognize that caregiving to frail elderly must always continue. But maintenance of health and finances is not the only aspect of older adult ministries. Making sure that the person is on an inner journey, the goal of which is to make faith more intentional, is important. Old age is not the enemy, but the attitudes that accompany aging are. Because the agenda of life changes in the later years, we need to think along new lines.

My informal research revealed that older adults are seeking for a place, a home, not just a spot to rest their bones. Their lives are as important to them as life is to a younger person. I hear repeatedly from this group that younger people are surprised to hear them say that their feelings are no different than when they were young. Falling in love is still an exciting experience.

A sound theology of aging will welcome older adults fully into the household of faith instead of directing them to the sidelines. That reorientation will require a major shift in the way we see and do church. My listening to older adults has showed me that they yearn for a clearly defined place and function that gives greater meaning to their lives. When you face the yield sign of aging, a reminder to older adults to allow a younger generation to move into the fast lane, it is important to keep affirming that life makes sense and has meaning even though death is closer and productivity lessened. Yet this means a shift in our way of seeing the world.

My months of writing led to renewal in my own life. Courage, strength, and joy grew with each month of working with the problems I set up. I found I was not tilting at windmills but at issues that many older adults face.

I do not claim to have come up with many answers. I am testing the waters. I merely state what I discovered. I live in an area where older adult ministries are as yet mostly a cloud on the horizon. The territory is big. The literature on the topic is extensive. The number of older adults is growing.

New models for looking at aging are developing in our society. God is doing a new thing with this generation of older adults who have received the gift of twenty to thirty additional years because of better health and technology.

Older adults once were highly respected and turned to for wisdom and advice. But their life knowledge became obsolete in a quick shift to high technology, and their experience was discounted as also out of date. Then youth climbed onto the pedestal and received the applause. But they have also tumbled from the high place once accorded them. The mature middle-aged adult with power, energy, and public relations skills is the model for today's society. But older adults, because of their increasing numbers alone, will force society to consider them more. When their time comes, they will need to have something to say.

—*Katie Funk Wiebe*
Wichita, Kansas
June 1994

BORDER CROSSING

1

Specially selected for you

You know you are old when the candles cost
more than the cake. —Selected

The bright red printing on the brown envelope said loudly, *Dear Shopper: Look inside for offers specially selected for you!*
The package had been sent from a large distributing house "specially" for me. Usually I throw such offers into the wastepaper basket. This time I slit open the heavy brown envelope and dumped out its contents—commercial coupons to be redeemed for the following products:
a laxative
arthritis pain medicine
denture adhesive
undergarments designed for leakage control
bran flakes
a specially designed chair for people with back
    problems
door chimes to extend the sound of the doorbell
magnifier for reading
card shuffler
side-cutting nail clipper
night driver glasses
specially designed slippers for people with feet

that change in size with the time of day
a hearing aid

As I flipped over the glossy four-color advertisements, I felt myself deflating like a punctured tire. If these
products were specially selected for me, who was I? What
was in store for me? I did not want to be the person having
to use these products, at least not all at the same time. But
obviously there was some connection between them and
my age.

A few years ago, I turned sixty-five. That was a big
event. No little glitch in the road, but an all-out welcoming
party to membership in the graying majority. Sixty-five
was a benchmark—no doubt about it.

My cousin Henry Funk sent me a specially designed
membership card, making me, with due pomp and ceremony, junior member of the senior division of the Funk
family clan. I felt almost as if I was being enrolled in an athletic club about to prepare for the Olympics. Now I know I
was.

My daughter Joanna, a graphic artist, sent me a personally designed card that stated,

> This is to certify that Katie Wiebe, having achieved
> sufficient experience and savoir faire, is now authorized
> to engage in spontaneous and outrageous behavior,
> including staying up past her bedtime, roaming the world,
> talking to strangers, and, of course, wearing purple whenev-
> er the mood strikes her.

She hadn't forgotten that I had once written that people would know I was old when I, like Jenny Joseph in her
popular poem, "When I Am Old," wore purple with a red
hat. Enclosed with her card was an outrageously beautiful
purple and red silk scarf.

The family threw a coming-out party at a specially-selected restaurant that caters to special events. No Mc-Donalds was considered for such an occasion. They produced flowers and presents. A video camera was used to immortalize for all time my shape, size, and hair color at this turning point in my life, as well as any pearls of wisdom that might fall from my newly aged tongue.

"Tell us stories we've never heard before," commanded son James, as he pushed a microphone in front of my mouth. He apparently expected me to press a button in my memory bank and start spouting stories of the olden days.

That fall every medical insurance company in the whole of the United States somehow learned about this sixty-fifth birthday and offered a still better deal in supplemental insurance.

Obviously I had arrived somewhere. But where was I? I didn't really know. Four years later, as I write this, I feel fairly comfortable with myself.

But I wonder about seventy and seventy-five. Sixty was merely fifty-five extended and sixty-five was sixty extended. But it is hard to see sixty-five and seventy as part of eighty and eighty-five. And, if the actuarial tables are correct and I have inherited my mother's genes of longevity, it is hard to imagine what the next twenty to thirty years will bring. Mother was alive and in fairly good health at ninety-eight. She died a year later, her health having suddenly given way to a variety of medical problems. Ninety-eight is a long time to be old and waiting for the next transition.

Moving across the border into old age is frightening because of its uncertainty. I admit it openly. Will I become a couch potato? Will I turn into a cranky old woman? I anguish over which of the numerous physical disabilities many older people experience will affect me. Hearing loss? (Noisy crowds bother me.) Eyesight? (I already wear trifocals. My mother had cataract surgery.) Arthritis? (Because I have tendinitis in one knee, when I get up from a kneeling position I look like a cow.) Loss of bone mass? (I broke an ankle last fall.) Forgetfulness? (Sometimes I can't remember which pocket of which coat I left my car keys in. Names of close friends may elude me.)

Most disconcerting is that I have little control over this cluster of losses. They invade and conquer without warning and without offering me a choice.

But what makes the journey into old age terrifying is that I hear no one beyond the middle years inviting me urgently and loudly to cross the border quickly because of its splendid advantages. A little child learning to walk has admiring fans in parents, siblings, and friends, cheering every faltering step. That cheering section was missing as I began to cross into the land of the aging. And that is the reason for this book.

I want a cheering section and can't find it. Therefore I want to learn how to cheer my own passage and that of others. And I can't before I know what I am cheering for.

The booing section is loud.

"I hate to think about growing old," said one friend.

"I don't even want to think about it," said another.

"Retirement scares me half to death," came from a professional.

"Retirement is most distressing," writes a retired minister. He feels shoved aside.

The newspapers carry their frightening articles about the elderly as sure suckers for bargains in shingling roofs or painting walls that turn into frauds. There are some cheery nursing homes. But one look into the front hall of other nursing homes removes all joy for the journey that lies ahead. A few of the frail elderly sit in an untidy row near the front entrance, head sagging, half-asleep, yet hoping for a visitor to offer a crumb of hope to brighten the day. Some nursing homes keep them carefully out of public view. In my head I know that only about 5 percent of older adults end up in nursing homes. In my heart I can't believe it.

Older adults—all kinds—need cheerleaders or advocates for their journey, just as adolescents need youth leaders to coach and cheer them on.

I want to be a cheerleader.

I want others to cheer me on.

I want this part of the journey to have dignity and hope. I want this border crossing; this time between citizenships; between social uselessness and non-identity, on the one hand, and conscious journeying, on the other; to be overwhelmed with grace and joy.

I am convinced that God must have something in mind for older adults, a role that the church is not talking openly about yet. I want to find out what that something is.

At that sixty-fifth birthday I knew there was no turning back. Each birthday would come and go with the regularity of a digital clock until the battery ran down.

Some of us grew into adulthood with the assumption that truth was received once and for all, then we adults were on a safe journey. We made spiritual decisions at camp, or at mother's knee, or at the church altar. In young adulthood we figured out whom to marry, what kind of job to work at, and what worldview to adopt.

Then some of us accepted that growth stopped. An adult was a finished product. Adults lived on a spiritual plateau until they died. We assumed middle-aged and older adults made few significant decisions or spiritual commitments to continued growing. Learning new facts and new approaches to living was not a viable consideration.

Amidst mail I received the year I was sixty-five was an invitation from a retirement center touting the many advantages of living there to enrich one's life. I found its message strangely unappealing as I read through this glossy four-color brochure. Then I figured it out.

This retirement center said much about what it did to provide topnotch meals, housing, exercise, and entertainment. It said little about how it encouraged residents to keep their minds stimulated and growing and to see themselves still on a journey, not coasting.

I also looked over a questionnaire prepared for church leaders seeking information about older members of the church. Again I was disappointed. The questions had mostly to do with maintenance-type issues, such as housing, finances, and health, and very little to do with the inner life, where the real battles of this transition are lost or won.

Though distributed through a church program, this public relations piece overlooked that older people have needs of the spirit, mind, and emotions—that part of life where the real crossing is made to being a confident church and family elder. It overlooked that women and men my age receive the gift of a new period in life that people didn't have fifty years ago—a gift of unmapped territory we are privileged to chart.

So I asked myself, What makes it hard to move into the land of the aging? Am I afraid that God will not come with me into this new stage of life? Why do I hesitate to step over the threshold? Why did the Israelites hold back at Kadesh-Barnea, the entrance to the Promised Land? Two of the twelve spies came back with positive reports about the possibility of overcoming the inhabitants. But the Israelites listened to the ten with the negative report. Were they afraid God wouldn't go with them down the valley into Canaan even though God had promised the land to them?

The ancient Canaanites worshiped gods of nature, fertility gods—in plain words, farmer gods. Baal was the god of earth and rain and sun, who ensured the rich harvest of grain. Were the Israelites troubled that Jehovah, who had provided manna miraculously in the wilderness, might not turn out to be like a Canaanite farmer god who could make crops flourish? In the wilderness, they hadn't learned to know God as an agricultural god who helped them with farming. In the wilderness God had worked miracles, producing manna, quail, and water—not a healthy stand of grapes or grain.

Older adults facing the threshold of this last stage have both conscious and unconscious fears that old age may yet offer the greatest test of faith. This is the time when real living begins, real in the sense that this is the run for the finishing line. Everything up to this point was preparation for the run toward the tape. Some admit their fears. Most don't. They know only that God's divine power, incarnate in human flesh through Jesus Christ, will be sufficient for the time when one is especially vulnerable to the body's frailties and the indefiniteness of each day's activities.

Some older adults feed their fears on rumors that the needs of their particular age group are beyond God's power to help. The enemies are too many—loneliness, ill health, sometimes poverty, physical and emotional neglect and abuse by children. And loss—loss of identity, of mobility, of friends, of family, of that wonderful sense of invulnerability we thrive on earlier in life. Stories of these losses are as plentiful as the many grumblings of the ancient Israelites.

Older adults are encouraged to believe also that the real answers to their numerous needs don't come through a healing or prayer service but from the government. Political clout alone may provide money and services to make life easier for them. Technology, not God and the Christian community, has the key to the problems of aging.

Older adults remember that the past, when they had a daily routine and went to work, was comfortable and manageable. Older believers know who God was in relationship to their life as a person fully engaged with family and society. But who is God now, in this new limited role as an elder?

At sixty-five I wasn't sure. Sometimes I felt as if life was closing in. I listened to older women who also lived alone speak about not driving in the city at night; about not going for walks alone; about spending days without talking to anyone; about getting no phone calls; about getting no mail.

Did I have the promise of God's continuing help and presence with each successive year? What would I do with the thirty years that lay ahead if I lived at least as long as my mother?

If sixty-five had felt like a step down (even with the big birthday bash), retirement from a fulfilling occupation a year later was a plunge to the basement level. A number of messages told me this in no uncertain terms.

The first message came through strong and clear. My work at the college where I had taught for twenty-four years was finished. The school showed appreciation for my past work by awarding me the professor emeritus title.

But I was now as free as a farm animal penned in a barn all winter, then loosed in spring in a pasture of several square miles. The feeling was both exhilarating and terrifying. The second message also rang clear. I might have retired, but society told me indirectly I should not think of myself as old or associate with the elderly, only with my own age group or those younger. I sense that some soon-to-be retirees consider old age a contagious disease, so they stay away from anyone whose hair is turning gray even if they're part of the same group. I cringed when people referred to my "retirement" as I sensed the meaning behind the words—used up, on the shelf, finished.

The underlying messages were obvious. To let yourself look old, talk about being old, or associate with the elderly and enjoy them was treason to self. To connect with the elderly—other than to acknowledge them as people you ministered *to* and cared *for*, not people you identified *with* and learned *from*—meant your own death knell socially.

At an aging conference, I noticed that the people present, many of whom were well over sixty-five, kept talking about the elderly as "they," never "us." As long as they could separate themselves from these "old" people, they seemed to think they could keep the birthdays at bay.

I bumped into the third unwelcome message about aging before long. Older people are not to be taken seriously. Older people are to be endured, physically and socially nurtured, perhaps pampered, and that's about it.

Some consider a person of sixty-five a spent person. It's as if the warranty for a meaningful life expires at that age. I've encountered the stereotypical view that being older means being passive and dependent and on a steady decline until you reach the final home base.

The fourth message was that old age and death are taboo subjects, even in Christian circles. Death and dying, going home to God the Father and Creator, isn't a welcome or open subject. Death means major defeat rather than joyous victory.

People like myself, standing at this threshold to a new period in our lives, are caught on a threshold. We're caught at a transitional point for which we think we've prepared ourselves. Yet we don't realize we haven't until we're actually there. We've told ourselves that we will work at projects postponed for years, and we assemble other grand strategies. But the real transition cannot be made until one is going through it.

And the transition must be made first in the spirit. Keeping busy with travel and other activities, as many retirees do, isn't the answer. Busyness only postpones facing the real inner transition of spirit and emotion and the opportunity for continuing growth. This busyness may be a defense mechanism to protect the need to kill time out of boredom, writes one gerontologist. Hanging desperately onto youth by use of cosmetics, surgery, and youthful clothing styles isn't the answer either.

A period of transition is a time of looking both backward and forward, not standing still. In transition there is movement. In retiring from teaching I had left one place, a conventional state of being, but had not yet arrived at another. I was between identities. And in the meantime I was experiencing some confusion, a sense of displacement, before I moved surely in a new direction. Like widowhood had been some thirty years earlier, this phase of life was a period of uncertainty and hesitation. Who was I? Where was I headed? I had a head answer but not a heart answer. But I was ready to learn. Because I was scared.

2

The eagle and the weasel

"Brave admiral, say but one good word:
What shall we do when hope is gone?"
The words leapt like a leaping sword:
"Sail on! sail on! sail on! and on!"
—Joaquin Miller, *Columbus*

Those of us who are growing older at the end of the twentieth century have watched our own parents, primarily our fathers, retire and move into new stages of life. Retirement is a fairly new phenomenon. Social security was only introduced in the 1930s to bring younger workers into the system and allow older ones to withdraw. Retirees weren't expected to live much past sixty-five.

From a distance of several thousand miles, I watched my father move from a world of work to a world of rest. Mother, never having worked outside the home, had fewer adjustments to make than Dad. She continued to do with joy what she had always been doing—cooking, cleaning, reading, sewing, and knitting.

For decades, Dad enjoyed being the manager of a corner grocery store in a small village in northern Saskatchewan. He got up early, before we children did, ate a hasty breakfast, and strode off to the store. From the upstairs bedroom with its slanting roof, I could hear his quick foot-steps on the wooden sidewalk alongside the house, followed by the gate creaking open and slamming shut. Dad never sauntered. He walked at a fast clip to face the tasks ahead—readying the store for the day's customers and serving the early buyers.

Though the store belonged to the OK Economy chain, community people knew it as "Funk's store" because Dad's stamp was clearly on it. He loved the store. Sometimes he could hardly tear himself away from it. Altogether he spent about forty years in that small red-brick building with the display posters and a few hastily built pyramids of boxes of soap flakes in the windows. The customers were his friends. His identity and self-esteem were wrapped up in that small store as securely as the customer's order of groceries was wrapped in brown paper and tied tightly with string.

His long-standing motto was that the customer was always right even if the customer was decidedly wrong. He catered to his customers, working hard to please each one. He gave them credit, sometimes for far too long so he was left holding the bill without hope of payment. He had groceries delivered for those who phoned in orders. That was my brother's job to do after school, using a bicycle or a wagon. The whole town wasn't more than five or six blocks long. My job as I grew older was to help behind the counter on Saturdays. All of us children helped fill shelves and count inventory. Our life as a family revolved around Dad's store.

Dad exchanged products for unhappy customers, even if they had eaten over half the jar of mayonnaise before pronouncing it inedible. He stored grocery orders along the wall while the owners shopped elsewhere or lingered at the local dance hall or beer hall. Closing time on a Saturday evening was often one o'clock or later in summer. Then Dad handed me a bottle of pop from the water cooler and sent me home, bone-weary.

He rejoiced when business was good and agonized when it was down and the stack of charge accounts grew thicker and thicker. He knew that some of these customers were not known for keeping promises.

The store was a gathering place for men, those without jobs, those between jobs, or those with nothing to do. In winter they would visit around the furnace register, its blast of hot air warming them in body and spirit. When business was slow, Dad joined the group discussions, dropping out to flip a feather duster over some cans, or to empty the receptacle that held the discarded pop bottle caps.

When the weather improved, the non-buying customers sat outside on the benches pushed against the brick front. All morning they cracked sunflower seeds, littering the sidewalk with shells. Then Dad would briskly sweep them up so they could begin again. He enjoyed sharing his store with people, for in doing so he was sharing himself.

As he grew older and his back became more bent, he tired of carrying out ninety-eight-pound sacks of sugar or flour. Mother's urgent request to use a cart or dolly fell on deaf ears. That wasn't manly. A real man carried the sacks out on his back with an energetic stride. He paid his female hired help less because they couldn't carry heavy sacks. He firmly insisted on equal pay for women if they could do men's work—lug ninety-eight pounds of flour.

At seventy he retired from his years of stooping, lifting, and carrying. He wanted and deserved an easier life. The energy was gone. He and Mother moved to the West

Coast, away from the bitterly cold, long winters of northern Saskatchewan. He wanted rest.

His first reports of retirement life were positive. He enjoyed having no daily responsibilities. He walked a great deal. He probably traversed every street in the city by foot.

He talked to all older people he met, particularly older men he found sitting on a street bench or in a park, idling away the day. "All old people here" was his frequent comment in letters to me about this retirement community nestled in the Fraser River valley.

He also wrote about the many lonely older people living there. Somehow he found them. Little clippings and sayings he enclosed in letters told me he was lonely, unsure of himself, unsure of what was expected of him now that he was a retired old man. The retirement honeymoon was over.

I had given him and Mother a book, *Conversations on Growing Older*, by C. Gilhuis. When, after his death, Mother returned the book to me, I noticed that he had marked passages like these: "For many people life before the door to eternity is a lonely life. . . . Yes, you sit in silence so much that the lively noise at a party or at a family gathering actually is a little too much for you." He underlined a passage that said that radio services and even the minister's visits—"if he has time—and does not forget you"—were no substitute for what one once "enjoyed, experienced, and received in this respect."

He also marked a passage that encouraged readers to live in and by the certainty that every day the Lord was with them. Dad, who had always been in daily contact with dozens of people, all of whom he knew personally, especially what they ate, was facing an unexpected challenge in the art of living and trusting in God, not his ability to work.

Unfortunately, Dad had never been a reader. He had never been one to participate with joy in formal visiting, where one made arrangements ahead of time, got dressed up and spent a stipulated number of hours in a home. His forty-some years as a shopkeeper had consisted of many little contacts with people, not prolonged sessions of talk. Dad had developed no hobbies, no compelling interests, other than to keep the store operating smoothly. And how he loved that store, especially when sales topped those of other stores in the same chain.

But time grew heavier and heavier on Dad's hands as walking became more difficult. Rest was becoming exceedingly boring. He had always had some artistic leanings, so he turned to painting by number but never made the switch to creating his own pictures. When the painting appeal palled, his interests migrated to textile painting and to knitting scarves on a small gadget.

We children carried home yards of cloth when we visited, for Mother to stamp patterns on for Dad to paint—only to keep him busy, not alive. In the first years, he did beautiful work, but at the end he painted only to get the task done, not because he enjoyed the work. It was something to occupy time. It did not feed his creative needs. He no longer knew why he was alive. I have often wondered why I, not he, wielded the pen, for he loved to tell stories, and when he preached as a lay minister, his sermons were chock-full of real-life illustrations.

Annie Dillard's opening essay in *Teaching a Stone to Talk* describes a meeting with a weasel, which led her to study weasels in greater detail. She learned that weasels are known for their tenacity of grip. In fact, an eagle was found dead in the wilds with the dried skull of a weasel still attached to its neck. Apparently the weasel had struck the eagle in a desperate attempt for food. The animal's teeth had sunk into the cartilage of the eagle's neck and was not dislodged even though the eagle flew off with the weasel in tow. Eagle and weasel died together, the eagle feeding on the weasel as long as it could to sustain life.

Annie Dillard asks whether she can sink her teeth into life with such tenacity—even if at the end it means being carried aloft as dried bones hanging from an eagle's underside. I thought of the weasel hanging tenaciously onto the eagle, even if it meant his death, and of my father—and of myself.

In his later years, Dad let go of the neck of the eagle. In fact, he had never reached for it after age seventy. *He didn't know he should.* From his own experience with older people, he knew old age only as a brief time to rest, sitting in the sunshine, cracking sunflower seeds and greeting the neighbors, before sickness and death interrupted, and God called the weary life-pilgrim home. People were old at sixty and died at seventy. He was planning to die, not to live a long time.

His mother, widowed since 1920, when her husband died of typhus following a short period of political imprisonment during the Russian Revolution, had been retired almost from the day she set foot on Canadian soil. That was in 1923, when she was fifty-one. She lived in this retired state until her death at age eighty-three. In her small weathered home, overgrown by hollyhocks in summer, she drank her endless cups of coffee and "neighbored," that beautiful Low German term that is hardly translatable.

Her example and that of other older people Dad had known, such as the men who sat in front of his store day after day all summer, had led him to believe that retirement meant relaxation and retreat, not reaching for life. He let the tension out of his life when he locked the door of the store for the last time. He was weary in body and in spirit. He wanted to do nothing.

In his younger years he was often desperately homesick for his homeland. My sister Anne remembers him rocking my baby sister's cradle and singing a Russian folk tune, tears streaming down his cheeks. Then Mother would cook him his favorite foods, like *Kasha* (fried boiled wheat) and *Kleetamousse* (milksoup with homemade noodles), foods his mother had cooked for him when he was a boy in South Russia. All his life he loved to listen to records of Russian national and folk songs sung in the minor key.

As a young man he had experienced service as a medic in World War I in Russia, working on a Red Cross troop train taking wounded soldiers back from the front. He also lived through the Russian Revolution and the famine and disease that followed, the memories of which came back to haunt him in increasing measure. These difficult memories, once pushed down and held back, now in old age refused to be chained any longer when there was too little to occupy his mind.

How many stories of violent bloodshed that disturbed his sleep and peace of mind did he take with him into the grave? Retirement for my father meant too much time to think about these agonizing memories of a land he had loved torn by war, bloody violence, political injustices, disturbed family structures, severe illness, and many family deaths. He had too much time to think of how as a younger man he had tried to cope and sometimes succeeded—and sometimes failed.

He spoke bitterly at times of the failure of his life. He

could list few accomplishments, economic or intellectual, as he saw them. That we children didn't judge him for this didn't seem to count.

In Blaine Lake, Saskatchewan, where we lived, he interacted with immigrant people like himself, who lacked a formal education, as well as with those who spoke English with finesse and had several academic degrees. His English skills had limitations, but his general zest for life, strong leadership ability, and readiness to risk had always carried him through many situations. This included functioning as village overseer, or reeve, for eight years. People spoke of him as the "town mayor," a term of respect.

But in old age, his inherent distrust of people in authority, acquired in South Russia, where the social division between landed and landless families was marked, increased and carried over to other people. He did business with banks only under duress, as a requirement of his responsibility as store manager. He never had a personal checking account, but preferred to carry cash in his pocket or pinned inside a jacket. This made him feel more secure; banks could go bankrupt.

He found it hard to ask people for favors or to accept them, especially for a ride to church after he had turned in his driver's license—even though he had driven untold numbers of people to their destination when he was driving. Attending public meetings became more and more of a burden. He frequently sat in the back row at the end so he could leave quickly. He withdrew more and more into himself.

The reward he expected for decades of hard work as a storekeeper was peace and rest, not continued engagement with life. That much-longed-for rest became an albatross around his neck, for he never expected to "rest" for several decades.

Twenty-one years after his official retirement, he died of a stroke at age ninety-one, somewhat embittered, withdrawn, never having reached for that which could have sustained him in his declining years. The depressed man I visited in the later years of his life was a sharp contrast to the vigorous man I knew as a child, the man who rose to each day's challenge with joy and abandon and came home with funny stories to tell about the life of a small-town grocer.

Dad never understood that retirement, a concept he had not known in Russia as a young man, meant hanging onto the tension in life. He never understood that retirement meant clinging to that eagle's throat even if it meant death.

Now I faced the unknown land of retirement and aging just as my father had several decades ago and as my children would after me. And I felt as if I was trying to leap across a wide chasm.

About five years ago, while visiting relatives in Germany who had recently migrated there from Russia under a repatriation plan, I attended a wedding with my aunt. After a lengthy service, we went to the reception and the program that followed in a congregation made up almost entirely of newcomers to Germany.

I watched with great interest as the bridal couple said a highly formalized farewell to their youth (*der Abschied er Jugend*). All their single friends filed past them on the platform to give them a farewell greeting. The bride and her young female friends wept as they kissed and hugged. The young men shook hands solemnly. All knew the new husband and wife were taking their places now in adult life. This Russo-German culture saw a definite dividing line between youth and adulthood.

And I sensed that our culture sees a similar division at retirement, with the retirement dinner substituting for the farewell service. At this juncture, work and/or career and retirement move in different directions.

With my purple scarf and my new title, professor emeritus, and freedom from the alarm clock, what did I want to do? What could I learn from my father's life? What did I want to be? What did I want to give to life? What should my agenda for living be? Clearly it could not be the agenda that had been mine in the morning of life. I had to change, but in what way?

I knew I wanted an identity, one of the greatest needs of people who have left the workplace and whose identity has been their vocation. I had been a college English teacher. What now?

I wanted to live with meaning and hope. I wanted to be able to cope with living alone, yet to know friends. I wanted to grow stronger in my faith and understanding of life, not dry up like a lemon left on the counter too long. And I didn't want to get shoved to the periphery of church life as I had seen happen to older adults in some congregations. I wanted the blessing of the Christian community, assuring me I did not necessarily have to do anything to be accepted as a member of that community. I was convinced that sometimes being old means just being.

And, oh yes, I wanted to have fun—to eat fewer beans and more ice cream. And to stay well. But it would mean clinging to the neck of the eagle even if meant risking death for life, terror for glory, risk for reward.

3

Galloping, naked, in the night

On life's vast ocean diversely we sail,
Reason the card, but Passion is the gale.
——Pope, *Moral Essays*

My daughter Christine moved from Chicago, where she had lived and worked for ten years, to Wichita, where I live, to be closer to family. The move was more traumatic than she had expected. One day, as we were having dinner together, she reflected that when a person moves from one locality to another, she loses her identity. Here in Wichita, no one knew the real Christine—creative, eager for friendships, highly motivated, organizer and list-maker, and lover of celebration and beauty. She was only a name, a blip on a mental screen, momentarily passing in and out of people's consciousness. Her self-esteem suffered as a consequence until she found her niche again.

Christine put into words some of my unspoken thoughts. After finishing twenty-four years of teaching at a small church college, I moved from a small community of three thousand to Wichita, an urban center with a population of over 300,000, to be closer to my children. In the little town I had an identity with most people as a single professional woman. In Wichita I was unknown in my neighborhood and in my church—probably another little single white-haired woman among other little single white-haired women expected to merge without a murmur into church life.

At any transition, such as marriage, parenthood, or new job, our self-identity is up for review. Moving into the junior branch of the senior division of the Funk clan meant a change in my identity in the eyes of family members. I perceived them as thinking that Aunt Katie, the teacher and writer, was now Aunt Katie, the *retired* teacher and writer who had joined the group of people saying publicly, "I have finished my main work in life."

For me this transition meant sorting through previous identities to see if I could find one I could accept now. But it also meant letting go of those previous roles and self-images that had once sustained me. It meant possibly accepting a brand new role and self-identity appropriate to this time of life. That looked like a terrifying challenge.

In *Looking Both Ways*, David J. Maitland advises that those facing a new stage in life should not let the discomfort of this transition pass without giving it attention. In other words, we shouldn't try to get over it like a cold, with lots of bed rest and fluids. He advises older adults to use this transition as one more chance at self-knowledge in an encounter with God. He speaks of this transition as God's invitation to move beyond preoccupation with one's self-image or identity (What am I now that I'm no longer a teacher?) to the search for self-knowledge. There is no way back.

I hesitantly accepted that my current discomfort with what was going on in my life existed to encourage me to find out more about myself and the passage I was entering. Struggling with holy discomfort hadn't been on my list of things to do as I adjusted to city living. Yet I tried to keep in mind the words of an older friend that old age is the proving ground of whatever one has believed, thought, and said.

The faith issue at transitions, Maitland writes, is the death of previous self-images for the sake of the possibility of the resurrection of a new image appropriate to the new age. But the transition is difficult because what we want to know about ourselves does not exist out there fully developed, like a new version of something already familiar. It became clear to me that the new identity I was looking for was not like the update of last year's car model. The emerging truth about myself might disturb me and take me in surprising directions.

I thought about Maitland's words for days. The death of old self-images he was referring to didn't mean discarding all previous identities. Rather, it meant sorting through previous roles and identities to find a new whole. I began to see that the process was like going through my clothes closet and taking a hat from one pile, a dress from another, shoes from yet another, and buying some new accessories, then discarding the leftovers. But even that wasn't a good enough analogy, for that was nothing more than a makeover of an old version of me.

Self-image, self-esteem, identity, or even the term *role*—these were not words I grew up with. Who worried in the depression and war years whether you had a good self-image or a bad one or whether you were fulfilling your role in life? There was no anguished daily measuring of self-esteem as there is today. We all knew people who were shy and withdrawn and lived on the fringes of life and also people who were loud-mouthed, mean-spirited, and obnoxious. These latter had "big heads," our parents told us. And then there were a lot of decent people in between who probably had reasonable self-esteem. Circumstances, very often, rather than personal decisions, determined what you did in life.

Looking back, I sense that I had a fairly good sense of myself, or self-image, using today's understanding of the term. The middle child, I wasn't given undue responsibility or excess babying. I did well in school, which helped my self-image. I could accomplish almost any academic task I was given and didn't give up trying until I had succeeded.

I enjoyed reading; in fact, I inhaled books. I became desperate if I didn't have a book to read, which happened often in that book-poor community. For me, one of the most wonderful moments of my childhood was to arrive breathless at the Searle Grain Elevator, which sponsored a rural lending library program, when the most recent wooden chest of books arrived. Often, in my presence, the elevator agent pried off the lid with a monstrous crowbar to uncover several dozen books. And I was first to choose a book. The moment was awesome. Excellent for the self-image.

The teen years passed without many upheavals. I became infatuated with one or more boys periodically, but since Dad and Mother had pronounced a no-flirting, no-dating ultimatum, the infatuation remained mine to dream about, not do anything about. I printed my name beside that of the current boy I liked, crossed out identical letters, then counted off the rest to "He loves me, he loves me not." Boys were such delightful creatures, and I think I saw myself as delightful too.

Somehow, when I was about sixteen, I managed to

scrape together enough money to buy a royal blue velvet beanie with two feathers sweeping high in the air. The hat rested confidently on my long, blonde, page-boy-styled hair, and the feathers danced jauntily as I walked. It attracted and aroused the passions of a young man I later couldn't get rid of, but I took pride in knowing it had attracted him. No poor self-image at this time either.

After high school I left home to attend a technical college to learn typing, stenography, and bookkeeping. The feathers on the hat and my spirit drooped during those months. I had wanted to attend university. But the schools weren't handing out humanities scholarships during the war years, only a few for study in military-related areas, such as the sciences. I received a small scholarship in physics when I wanted one in the humanities. I declined it.

Teachers had tried to dissuade me from going to a technical school to learn typing and shorthand. Anyone could do that. I had been awarded the governor-general's medal for all Saskatchewan the summer of my senior year in high school. It told me I had potential. I had a future. But potential needs money and my family had none. Business school and sitting at a typewriter, transcribing someone else's words, seemed like a life sentence.

I gritted my teeth as I studied Gregg shorthand and took speed typing tests to get out of that technical institute as quickly as possible. I had determined that business courses were for the less able student. And I was smart. As soon as a student's skills were up to a certain level, he or she could leave. When I could type eighty words a minute on a manual typewriter and take shorthand at 120, I left to take myself off Dad's hands, who I knew was sacrificing to enable me to get even six months' education in this institution.

But that still didn't mean much. I endured four months of being an order clerk for a meat distributing plant. My self-image plunged even lower. The good life was not coming as fast as I had expected. My job was to accept telephone orders for meat products such as bologna, wieners, lunchmeat. I have described myself elsewhere as being a "bologna god." When it came to distributing this much-wanted type of cold cut, I had full jurisdiction.

Sitting in my cubbyhole, perched on my stool, I read the help-wanted ads and plotted how to get out of this humiliating experience, where my co-workers were rough-and-ready workers, albeit good-natured and given to much teasing. In a few months, I had located a legal secretary's job in a downtown office. No more bologna-god life for me.

I became a bookkeeper/stenographer. I worked lawyer's hours, which meant an extra fifteen minutes at noon and shorter hours in summer when the court was not in session. I learned how to file, take shorthand for several days to have plenty to do when my employer was gone, keep the firm's books, type accurately even with fifteen carbons, and accept responsibility. I was in charge of the office when my lawyer/employer was absent. To this day I can hardly slit open an envelope without automatically turning it inside out after I have taken out the letter to make sure nothing else is enclosed.

Good self-image? Clearer identity? Yes, I think so. I learned I could handle responsibility for the entire office, even dealing with older employees. I was respected for what I could do and gained a great deal of self-respect.

I didn't enjoy one aspect of the work in this law office because it took me back into that aspect of life I was trying to move above—lower-class poverty. It was also my first encounter with the elderly poor. Once a month I was assigned to collect rents at an ancient tenement house our firm managed, occupied mostly by single male old-age pensioners.

When I entered the battered tin-covered building, I first knocked at the door of cheerful, chubby-cheeked Tom Wilkinson, resident caretaker. He reminded me of a weathered cherub who had stepped out of a Charles Dickens novel. He pushed his fat little legs up and down the halls hollering, "Rent! Rent!" while I, in the role of official rent collector, seated myself at a paint-chipped table shoved against the burlap wainscotting to wait for the tenants. I felt as if I also had stepped out of a Dickens novel.

One by one the men, often unshaven, shuffled toward my table in their worn slippers, wearing nondescript pants over graying long-handled underwear and no shirt, to hand me their six or seven dollars, all in one dollar bills or change. Sometimes they were embarrassed to find a young woman acting as landlord this month. They returned to their small cubicles to lie on narrow cots and listen to the radio and heat a tin of soup or beans on a kerosene burner.

That period of nearly three years after high school was fairly directionless, yet lived in a happy-go-lucky style. I had no goals because I wasn't actually expected to have any. And anyway, a young woman's main aim should be to find a husband.

I was treading water, waiting for romance, marriage, and family—until the Christ of the Damascus road caught up with me and asked me who was Lord of my life. I turned in a different direction. And the much dating, movie-going, and activity for activity's sake became not so much wrong as meaningless. Knowing the direction one is going does wonders for one's identity. I left the law firm and went to Bible college for two years to learn more about God's Word and ministry.

My study of myself shifts to the time I became a wife, shortly thereafter a mother, and then, after fifteen years, a widow and single parent at age thirty-eight. I recall one new widow lamenting to me she didn't want to be called the humiliating term "widow." Yes, widowhood was a stepping down, back, and away from society. Earning a living for a family of four children, going to school, and looking after the children meant daily encounters with few successes and many defeats.

My self-esteem dipped to its lowest as I recognized I was viewed as "a poor widow with four young children," with emphasis on the "poor" and "young." Every story and novel I had read about widows and experiences I had had with them came to mind. None were good. And I shuddered to think that this might be my identity until I died.

Many widows struggle with finding a new social role as a manless woman in a coupled society. I struggled mostly with discovering who I was when I was no longer Mrs. Walter Wiebe (the way married women were known in those days), under my husband's loving care and protection.

The question I am most often asked is what kind of person I would have become had my husband lived. The questioners are thinking of widows they know who have blossomed after their husband's death. I don't know the answer. I hope I would have grown and developed my gifts. But it is also possible I might have been content to hide behind my husband's role and position.

With my husband's death, I had lost my own identity

as surely as if I had lost my name. Looking back to those days, I see a woman who was determined not to stay on the bottom rung but who crawled two steps forward and one step back until gradually I began to forge a new identity as a college teacher and a writer on serious topics.

Now out of these various identities, what have I learned about myself? Self-evaluation is more than accumulating a record of experiences, like a collection of salt and pepper shakers, but evaluating them and learning from them. As I rethink my adult life, I acknowledge I once looked down on anyone who was single, poor, scholastically disadvantaged, and old. I didn't want to associate with such people lest some of what they were might rub off on me. My attitude changed, however, when I was single again, living on a limited income, vocationally disadvantaged, and socially a leftover in a coupled society.

In Peter Shaffer's play, *Equus*, Martin Dysart, a psychiatrist, is trying to learn why his young disturbed patient blinded the eyes of several valuable horses with a metal spike. He learns that, before the blinding incident, the boy occasionally took the horses at night to the shore and raced them, bareback and naked, at top speed.

The boy has been telling Dysart, "At least I galloped. When did you?" The psychiatrist is forced to acknowledge that the boy did something he had never allowed himself to do—know passion. He tells Alan's parents, "He was dangerous, and could be again, though I doubt it. But that boy has known a passion more ferocious than I have felt in any second of my life. And let me tell you something: *I envy it.*"

At least for one hour when the young boy was racing along the shore, Alan was living with passionate freedom, "howling in a mist," freed of the inhibitions of the common round of life. The psychiatrist had lived with boredom and routine, never approaching the edge. He hadn't kissed his wife in six years. The boy's actions asked questions he had avoided all his professional life.

I recognize now, as I look back over my many experiences, that I have known too much fear. I have been too hesitant at times to move ahead. I have seen a ferocious lion behind every blade of grass. Something of my father's apprehension about other people and how they might respond to me has rubbed off like indelible ink. Reading books about aging causes me to believe that many older people regret that, to keep life controllable, they lived life too cautiously, held their cards too close to their chests.

I wish now I had had more courage to move forward decisively and been less concerned about what the church community would think of some of the vision I felt entrusted with. I wish I had written more frankly, more furiously, more forcefully. And yet I know readers have told me that they have admired my gutsiness in opening issues, reaching for truth. But only I know how much I held back —deleting words, lines, paragraphs—to keep myself in safe harbors.

If I have learned anything about myself as I look back, it is how little I have galloped at breakneck speed, how little I have known passion for truth and justice, not even as my father knew passion for the downtrodden. When he saw suffering, he hurt with the person and did what he could to help with his limited means. He anguished over the violence and killing in the world but felt helpless and sometimes concerned about what the people would think of him, an uneducated immigrant storekeeper, speaking out. I, a woman in a man's church world, was also afraid of "What will the people think?" I very much wanted to be liked.

At times I spoke out against issues I felt strongly about, but not with the boldness of a Martin Luther King, Jr., or an Archbishop Romero, or even a Maggie Kuhn (who founded the Gray Panthers). My concern about the inadequacy of either/or answers, about the cruelty of intolerance, about the chains of rigidity, was sometimes lost between the lines. Kierkegaard said, "Reflection is usually the death of passion." Was my inherent reflective nature the leaching of my passion?

I recognize I may not have celebrated with lavish measure the beauty and glory of God, of God's creation, of life and love and beauty and truth. Too often I was thinking only about getting through the day, of dealing with my unique pain. And like others I became outraged, not at important things, but at the length of boys' hair and girls' skirts, at the preemption of a favorite television program for sports, or at the dog barking next door all night.

Yet as I stand before my life, I know that the mark of maturity means to give assent to the givenness of one's life—one's experience, one's skills, one's reputation, one's pain and losses, what one has or has not achieved. To do so means having achieved what Erik Eriksen refers to as *integrity*, a trait of the older adult.

I watch older adults who have achieved a tranquillity about life that exudes great strength, confidence, and peace of mind. They have discarded the agendas to act, to produce, to fill time, which society imposed on them in their early years. In old age they have accepted their lives as they were and kept moving on from there. They have continued growing God's image in themselves.

I can't live my life again. I can't redo it. Nor did I do it alone. God graciously used my weaknesses and strengths, my successes and my failures. There were times when I spoke for truth with the only measure of passion I could gather. Sometimes the vision I traveled with was meager and dim, sometimes more fully focused. Sometimes I was inspired, and people wrote me to thank me for my vision.

But sometimes life moved along happenstance. I can't identify all circumstances as God's work or as miraculous answers to prayer. But I can say that my journey thus far was an earnest attempt to live with and for God. And that will also be enough for this border crossing.

Society urges even older adults to adhere to a certain mold—to consume heavily even if they can't produce as much, to withdraw gently and silently to the periphery with their hoard of the world's goods, and generally to match the image of "old" as depicted in the media. But what I as an older adult need is a continuing vision of God and God's kingdom and the realization that change can take place year by year—but only if I accept that it can take place. Otherwise, I yield to society's image of the older person as someone who changes only in the opposite direction, becoming more neurotic, contentious, and dissatisfied with the years. That also is change.

Paul Tournier writes in the *Seasons of Life*, "If living means choosing and if in adulthood this is true to an ever greater degree, then choosing becomes the supreme vocation of old age, when life has become privation and earthly treasures have lost their glitter."

My life is my responsibility—not my parents', children's, friends', or society's. But with this transition I have another chance to escape bondage to past agendas, some culturally imposed, and, accept a better understanding of who I am and who I may still become as an elder. When we move through a transition to a new role, even when we are older, we have an opportunity to find out how we can become more like God, or, in simpler terms, how we can become more holy or righteous. Old age is real living.

We all cheer for favorite teams. But it is also important to cheer for ourselves as we move through life. Every time we get the ball and head for the basket, we need to cheer our own action. It means praising God for ourselves. As I think through my border crossing, I see myself more and more in training as a cheerleader, not only for older adults, a group whose cheering squad has too few members, but also for myself. And I wonder if this age group has the secret urge to ride bareback in the night, on the shore, naked, unencumbered by the stigma of ageism church and society has placed upon us.

4

Between a rock and a sure place

Beyond the great things we cannot do and the small things we will not do, the danger is that we shall do nothing. —Monod

Sunday mornings, when I was a child, our family of two adults and five children piled into the 1929 McLaughlin Buick (purchased secondhand from Dad's employer). Mother and Dad and one young child filled the front seat. Three children jammed into the back seat with cornflakes boxes and rags close at hand for those who had problems with motion sickness (me). One child perched on an improvised jumpseat (our lunchbox).

Our destination was twenty miles over dirt roads across the river to worship among "our people." Only we didn't talk in terms of "worship" in those days, but simply of "going to church." Worship was what people in cathedrals engaged in, not what we attended.

However, (and this was a big HOWEVER), we went to the little white frame church across the river only if the weather looked as if it would remain sunny and dry all Sunday. Father never relaxed in church if even a cloud the size of hand appeared on the distant horizon. For him it spelled trouble, not Elijah's proof of God's being with him.

Sometimes, despite Dad's eagle eye on the weather, we got caught in a rainstorm away from home. At once the upper layer of the gravel and dirt roads turned to a gray-brown slime. The happy atmosphere in the car turned deadly serious as if by remote control. No more singing. No more laughing. Each child knew the TERRIBLE THING that might happen—the Funk family might land in the ditch. And then what would we do? And where would we go to the bathroom if there wasn't a bush in sight?

At such times, the muddy roads required all the driving skills and patience of the Guardian and Protector of the Funk Family. All of Mother's unwavering support of the Guardian and control of her brood were tested by her physical endurance—one hand always reached behind her and held the lock down on the back door—and by her emotional stamina.

"Children, be quiet," Mother admonished frequently. As if we'd say anything.

We knew Dad was tackling Mount Everest. And none of us had safety belts and hobnailed boots. More likely we were wearing our best dresses with big bows around our waists and in our hair, and Sunday shoes on our feet— hardly fit attire for tackling the slippery mountain of mud.

Driving up the hill on the far side of the river after having crossed the river by ferry was like Sisyphus' rolling the rock up the hill, only to see it descend once he got it there. The car lurched a few feet ahead, only to slip and slide as the engine lost power.

But then it was Mother's turn to act. She ungartered her stockings (discreetly, of course) and removed them and her shoes. She quickly stepped into the muddy slime, found a good-sized stone in the ditch, and placed it behind a back wheel. This gave Dad a chance to get his foot off the brake, rev the motor, and try again.

The car chugged ahead a short distance, while Mother waited behind with the stone, trying to stay out of the slipstream of mud, ready to place it behind the wheel when the engine died out a second time. Maybe even a third time and fourth time. We always made it home.

When I finished teaching at Tabor College and settled in seriously to being "retired," I often wished someone would place a rock behind one of my wheels to keep me from sliding downhill. I was facing my own Mount Everest, although I thought I had prepared for this new period in my life. I had some unwritten goals for what I wanted to happen when I resigned from my teaching position at Tabor College. Like a puppy nibbling at my heels, they had been bothering me for several years as I went about my daily teaching duties.

1. Sleep later in the mornings. No more 7:30 a.m. classes.
2. Drink brewed coffee, even if decaffeinated, and read the paper each morning.
3. Learn to know my grandchildren.
4. Volunteer instead of responding only to requests.
5. Exercise, exercise, exercise. And learn to swim.
6. Finish writing projects started years ago.
7. Study the Bible more.
8. Continue speaking engagements.
9. Revive some crafts I did years ago. And relearn to cook.
10. Continue nearly everything else I was doing except grading freshman English composition papers.
    Queen Elizabeth of England has her boxes of documents to sign that accompany her wherever she

goes. I had my stack of freshman essays. And I groaned more and more with each year when I viewed the high pile that would occupy my evening and weekend hours.

And now I was free of them.

But free for what? Free to slide down the hill?

One evening I attended a meeting of people interested in starting a support organization for the local library. Fifteen to twenty people attended, mostly women, mostly retirees. The head librarian did a fine job of introducing the topic—library support. But the speakers, a retired business couple, were something else. She was chirpy, bright, energetic; he had a loud, harsh voice. Both overburdened us with details about ways to make money for the library instead of inspiring us to work for it. We could sell plants, bumper stickers, wind socks, home cooking, etc., etc.

When they finished their tempest of information, the upshot was that no one present wanted to start a new fundraising organization with officers, bylaws, and so forth. They were willing to help in less commercial ways.

I went home feeling strangely empty. Had I retired from teaching to shelve books and do shelf-reading? Or to sell bumper stickers? And I knew that this kind of invitation would be repeated as organizations became aware I had discretionary time. I began to grasp that some people expect the retiree's role to be to raise funds for significant causes through little insignificant projects, or to do those tasks that consume too much of the manager's time.

"Mother, where are you? Take off your stockings and get out. I need a rock behind my wheels!" I cried inwardly. I was starting to slip down the hill, for the engine was giving out. The feeling of pressing forward was gone, because it seemed clear that people who one day are doing significant work teaching, running a business, or managing a factory are expected to drop to the end of the pack the next. And that first year of retirement I accepted that that was the way it had to be.

Why did I believe this? Because nearly everyone said something in their congratulatory remarks about retirement being a time to grow lazy and watch the grass grow.

Unless I got out and put a rock behind my own wheels, I would slide. And for a while I couldn't find one.

In the back of my mind, I was seriously contemplating a move from Hillsboro, where we as a family had lived for nearly thirty years, to Wichita, about fifty-five miles away. The children had all left home; two of them and their families were living in Wichita at the time. A third would move there a year later.

The act of shifting residences was not the rock I was looking for, but it did become a small stone. It forced me to think through the years that lay ahead. When I finally moved, a year after retirement, I answered many questions about my reasons for leaving a peaceful rural retirement center for the unknown evils of the big city, where violence and crime seemed out of control.

Why did I leave Hillsboro? I had considered the situation of my own parents, who retired a thousand miles away from close family members. For some years this worked well. But when their health deteriorated, my sisters in Canada had to make frequent and sometimes inconvenient trips to the West Coast to attend to their needs. I didn't want that to happen to me. I wanted to spend the last years close to my children, although I know not all children look after aging parents. I trusted mine would, for I had seen them come through beyond expectations during other family health crises. They would do so again.

Furthermore, I knew myself. I needed encouragement to stay involved rather than to drift toward the disengaged life. Retirement communities, such as the one I had been living in, sponsor many activities to keep older people busy, but too few that challenge them to transcend themselves. I had watched several of my friends floundering in search of a new foundation for their lives.

But a year later, in the city, I had to admit I had been naive about my plans for the future, most of which were geared to keeping my wheels churning, not getting me up the hill.

Old patterns are hard to break. Shifting from full-time daily involvement in an institution to self-initiated activities would not be without *Sturm und Drang*. One newly retired professional man told me, "I feel as if I have a one thousand-horsepower engine inside of me, and I'm being asked to do a one hundred-horsepower job." Another told me of not sleeping at nights in his struggle to understand his strange feelings at not being a productive member of the work force. Retirement was not a stimulating experience initially for the two men. I watched an older couple travel thirty miles weekly to the next community to find satisfying volunteer activities.

After my move I learned to my chagrin that I was still very much the person I had been in Hillsboro, someone who likes to get up early and get going even without 7:30 a.m. classes. I am a morning person.

I still hate exercising.

My direction-finding skills are still nonexistent, yet one reason I moved now rather than later was to learn to drive with confidence in the city. The first weeks, and even months, I sometimes wandered around the Riverside area where I live trying to find a straight street to take me home.

I still get lost when streets don't run north and south and east and west, like decent streets should, and the sun isn't shining.

I learned to an even greater degree that growing older (never old) is a process, not an event. Retirement may be a single ceremony ushering one with fanfare and flowers into a new phase of life, but it is only society's way of saying, "We're sending you on your way with our blessing. Now it's up to you. No one is going to check on you to see if you get up in the morning or sleep all day. It's your life. And you may have to place rocks behind your own wheels."

We much prefer to have someone order our lives, whether through remunerative work or committee assignments. Having an assignment gives authority to what we're doing. What a difference to have to decide the activities of an entire day, day after day, and an entire life, year after year, without someone pushing or calling, and knowing that this will continue until death. Retirement means becoming entirely your own authority.

Some of my initial goals were superficial at best, nothing more than time-fillers. They needed to be exchanged for a larger vision of the purpose of life as an older person. I had thought a lot about retiring but not about what God's plan was for the older person. I didn't have a well-considered approach to aging. I had closed my mind to the understanding that God is doing a new thing with older adults in our generation.

My age group is faced with an unplanned-for twenty to thirty years after age sixty or sixty-five which we may not have counted on. Consequently, we may fall into ruts instead of discovering new life patterns that will make this period meaningful. Older adults have gained from medical advances but have lost because the quality of their lives has not always improved. People are living longer and not knowing why. Betty Friedan writes in *The Fountain of Age*, "Women and men have to break through the narrow vision of the dread mystique of age" and see "these new years of human life as uncharted territory for human evolution."

What faced me first when I moved to Wichita was selecting from a variety of time-fillers. Sometimes it was difficult to recognize them as such because they all came with glorified labels: volunteer work or older adult activities. I began the sorting process.

"The only answer to the age of anguish is a sense of significant being," writes Rabbi Abraham J. Heschel.

> The sense of significant being is a thing of the spirit. Stunts, buffers, games, hobbies, slogans are all evasions. What is necessary is an approach, a getting close to the sources of the spirit. Not the suppression of the sense of futility, but its solution; not reading material to while away one's time, but learning to exalt one's faculties; not entertainment, but celebration are approaches.

Strong words. I needed them.

With those words firmly in mind, I realized that even shelf-reading might eventually find a place. Basically what I had to do was push against the retirement mentality of withdrawal, of slowdown, of bowing out of life as long as I had strength and mobility and a clear mind.

To a certain degree, I faced what I had faced when I became a widow some thirty years before. It took me a while then before I sensed I needed a spiritual and psychological approach to being a widow. I needed to do more than tend to the unexpected day-to-day needs, like repairing the muffler on the car or figuring out how to relight the pilot light on a recalcitrant furnace.

Now I had to tell myself again—any transition, whether widowhood or aging, challenges a person to surrender security in earthly things, to trust deeply in God, and to move on. The rocks needed behind the wheel will show up. My task is to keep the car moving forward, even if very slowly. Life is a series of puzzles, or ambiguities, and we must keep working at them. It is a spiritual task, it is a theological task, it is an emotional task. What is necessary is "getting close to the sources of the spirit."

So how does one approach aging with a spirit of joy, hopefulness, and meaning? I watch some retired friends become superactive in travel, volunteering, attending meetings, and such activities. They exclaim, "I don't know how we got everything done when we were working!" I don't want to be judgmental, but I feel that some of that intense activity may prevent a person from reflecting on and thinking through an approach to this last stage in the life cycle that will undergird all of doing and being.

My primary goal is to arrive at integrity, to find out how all of life fits together from the perspective of a greater distance then when it started. In old age meaning is not achieved by what a person does or produces but through what the person is. Old age can continue to be a time of spiritual growth and rediscovery of spiritual truths.

Boundaries of the meaning of life can continue to expand even when physical boundaries are growing more restrictive. But for this to happen, there needs to be a spiritual community or support group which shares the values of the older person. Such a support group is worth more than two or three superficial friendships.

Where to find that group? In several congregations I

was familiar with, I sensed the older group felt shoved aside—not an unusual experience. Some openly told me so. I wondered why. They were rarely visible in leading any aspect of public worship, nor were their activities and volunteer contributions mentioned in congregational newsletters. No one joined these groups. An invisible wall had been erected around them. Their members were growing older and leaving the group through death, but the age-group immediately below them, and sometimes even members of their own age, stayed away from them. Was it because it might taint them with the kiss of death?

To identify with older adults places you in the group of those who may have physical and emotional limitations and who are stereotyped as cranky, inflexible, forgetful. Yet old age has many stages, and people of any one age may differ vastly. Each stage asks the individual to let go and move on—to push into the unknown, acknowledging the losses but without giving into them and giving up. Growing older means learning to become good at giving up in some areas to gain new strengths in others.

But being good at giving up doesn't mean sliding backward down the hill in the mud. Doing must eventually give way to being, for identity does not come from what one did or what the children do or even what one would like to do. Placing the rock behind the wheel means taking personal responsibility for one's life.

Perhaps we need formalized courses in aging before the time comes, just like we need need help in parenting. On-the-job training for growing old is not always sufficient. This is because the degree to which older adults are involved in their own aging is determined by the degree of self-motivation, which sometimes slackens as life becomes thin.

Where to find this self-motivation? One of my chief sources of encouragement to get on with life is the example of other older people like Elbert C. Cole, founder of the Shepherds' Care Centers of America.

At a conference on aging held at Messiah College, Grantham, Pennsylvania, in the spring of 1992, Cole stated boldly, "The faith community has the missing piece in an aging society." Its role should be to build in a challenge to older adults that there is life ahead. It has a theological task to accomplish—to answer the question of what God has in mind for the older adult and to help older adults develop a vision for life.

Cole pointed out that when the topic of the older adult comes up, attention shifts almost immediately to those who are dependent and living in nursing homes or confined to their own homes. The focus is on the minority of the elderly who are frail and have serious needs but who still live mostly in their own homes. Only about 5 percent live in nursing homes. We do not focus on the majority of the elderly who have energy, time, skills, and often discretionary funds to offer church and community.

The faith community, he said, too frequently raises the question of maintenance issues when it should be raising questions of purpose of life and attitude toward it. He insisted that the future of the church is in the hands of the older adults, not the young people. Older people determine how the younger generation will face old age. They provide role models for them in aging. And part of the difficulty is that my generation had too few really older people to use as models when we were young. The old died at that time when they were sixty and seventy.

A church with mostly older people is not a dying church, as some infer. The church must show society that faith makes a difference in the older years. People should continue to make new discoveries about faith as they grow older, and that is the challenge to pastoral leaders. The task of the church is never done until a person dies.

Here I identified one of the main reasons I left the community where I had taught for many years. The congregation was not challenging the older adults to keep making new discoveries about faith. The focus was on children and young people and families. That is an important emphasis, as it is in the congregation I joined in my new home. But now I knew what I wanted.

Cole inspired me. He put another stone behind my wheel. I took new courage and hope. I decided to replace my original behavioral objectives with broader goals—

• I accept that God has plans for the older adults. I don't know the details but I'm ready to start working at them.

• I accept the goal of lifetime learning as long as I have ability and strength. I won't always feel inspired and willing, but this is my goal.

• I want to make myself responsible for the elderly who are in nursing homes or are shut-ins in their homes or other institutions. My immediate response to this goal was to volunteer for Hospice, an organization that ministers to the needs of the dying in their own homes or in homelike institutions.

• I want to care more for God's world by the way I use its resources. Recycling is a headache in a home without room for bins, but I started a compost heap and placed boxes in the garage for recycling plastics and glass. I hope my zeal will last.

• I want to share whatever wisdom I have gathered through the years by telling my story, the stories of my family, and the stories of others who have shared their stories with me. Senior adults have had unique experiences. They are a church's biggest resource for practical wisdom.

• I want to become more involved in my own health care. I want to ask more questions when I go to the doctor.

• I want to join the faith community more confidently, even as a single older woman, a member of a group that frequently gets shunted to the widows' bench. I want to help other single women do the same.

The motivation to retire is often to join the RV brigade and head for places where the sun shines more often. Yet I sense that the goal should be to join a welcoming faith community, not to withdraw. The faith community needs to be the focus of what constitutes quality living.

• I want to make my faith life more intentional and encourage others to do the same.

David J. Maitland writes that to grapple intentionally with the ambivalences of every life stage is "the ordinary means by which the question of Christ's lordship is encountered" (*Looking Both Ways: A Theology for Mid-life*). To deny or disregard the ambivalences accompanying aging results in a rejection of the opportunity for growth.

The journey had begun. The weather wouldn't always be sunny, but I was better prepared for mud on the hill. I knew where to find the rocks.

5

Growing up Christian, growing old(er) Christian

Growth is the only evidence of life.
—John Henry Newman

Before I hopped onto the swing, I unhooked my garters. In a few seconds my uncomfortable lisle stockings had become neat brown doughnuts around my ankles. I knew I'd have to pull my stockings up before I went into the house, but why wait to feel the delightful freedom of bare legs after months of long underwear, heavy stockings, and knee-high boots? I pumped the swing back and forth vigorously. Summer would soon be here.

When I was a child, summer activities lined up in my mind like goslings behind their mother at the first hint of spring. My sisters and I usually trudged to a small nearby slough to collect tadpoles. I had already saved several low tin cans, like sardine tins, for making mud pies. My friend and I decorated them with small stones, seeds, flowers, and fine sand. Then we baked them in the sun. Maybe Mona and I could make ourselves some new horsehair rings when the ranchers again corralled their wild horses in the next block.

Yes, I was waiting for summer, but I and many others

waited for much more those years of the Great Depression in northern Saskatchewan.

The much needed rain to fill the slough never came. As we played in the dusty corner lot, the dry grass and weeds crackled beneath our feet. Dad's worry lines deepened as the bills spiked on the kitchen cupboard grew in number. Fewer and fewer of his store customers paid with money; more and more handed over relief vouchers.

As I think about growing up Christian in my small home community of Blaine Lake, Saskatchewan, I recall that each morning during the Depression years my little red-haired immigrant mother, after she had read us a Bible story, prayed as always in German, "Thank you, Lord, for food, clothing and shelter. Give us this day our daily bread." We children slid over our table prayers to get at the food faster, but she prayed slowly, deliberately, as if she were talking to someone. And that memory had a greater influence on me than many eloquent verbalizations by important theologians.

During those long, dry summer days, I watched the freight trains rumble by our backyard. At first, only a few men lay on the train roofs, then more and more. One day as I trudged to the store, a group of them had found their way to the bench by the bank building. Cautiously I eyed the empty, waiting faces. They didn't belong in my world.

But they entered it anyway. One early afternoon, someone knocked at the kitchen screen door. "Mom, come, there's someone here!" I called as I stared into the face of a hobo. Solemnly he handed Mother a note from my father in the store. "Give this man something to eat, and then let him chop some wood."

She invited him in, showed him where to wash, and prepared some food. She set the table as carefully as she would have for us and served him standing, as was her old country custom when guests were present.

I watched from the doorway. He smelled rank. His clothes looked grimy and worn. Why had Dad picked him? After eating hungrily, he chopped some wood and left.

Those years I understood too little about Mother's life a decade earlier in the Ukraine. She and many others struggled through the Russian Revolution (1917-19) and its violent aftermath of disease, famine, death, and dislocated families. Most of her immediate family had stayed behind when she and Dad emigrated to Canada. Some had died because of deprivation of basic needs.

I understood little about basic Christian doctrines and theologies and the giving and living a local congregation expected of its members. I saw only my parents, two people who were not adjusting easily to a new country. Mother told me often when I was an adult how terribly lonely she had been those first years with five young children and no English language skills. Yet I understand now that the actions of others have a large part in forming our theology even into our latter years, sometimes more than what we are directly taught.

Something happened as I watched the homeless man eat at our table. I was no longer waiting. Sharing our family's "daily bread" with him, the bread Mother prayed for, made life whole for a moment. This was what Mother was praying about.

This man was not the only stranger to sit at our table or sleep in our beds during the 1930s. But I shall never forget him, sitting at the head of our table, silently eating our food, and Mother serving him as if he were an invited guest.

I understood Mother's words much better the next morning as she again prayed, "Thank you, Lord, for food, clothing, and shelter. Give us this day our daily bread." Now I knew she wasn't just saying words.

My parents talked little about their inner lives. Their European background made it difficult for them to talk about faith and feelings. You could preach about that, but you didn't express emotion openly to one another. You didn't talk about your "relationship with Christ," although you did confess whether you were "a believer." You quietly lived out your faith.

In Russia a confession of faith had sometimes resulted in economic and physical harm, even death. A sister and her husband had been exiled to the north because he was a minister of the gospel. The glibness with which people today announce, "The Lord told me to do this," or "The Lord answered my prayer," as if they spoke to God on a cellular phone, was not part of my growing up. Incidents like the one with the hobo were what drew me to the Christ my parents believed in.

I don't want to give the impression that we were without religious training. Christian teaching was there, but it was implicit rather than explicit. We learned lessons in ethics every day—honesty, punctuality, faithfulness, generosity, and trust in God. We probably spread our church attendance too thinly over too many churches to feel loyal to any particular one.

In summer, for a few months after the ice in the river thawed and the ferry was put back in service, we attended a Mennonite Brethren church across the river. I think we sort of knew that this was "our" church. But the one we attended and enjoyed more because we knew it better was the United Church of Canada, with its less confining views about the Christian life. Hellfire and the wrath of God weren't often mentioned here. We were supposed to love God and do good.

"G-double O-D, good," we sang loudly in Sunday school. "I will try to be like Jesus, G-double O-D, good." Only much later did I learn that this was rank "liberal" teaching. Salvation was by grace, not by works.

Sunday school took place at 11:00 o'clock on Sunday morning in the one-room white frame United Church building with green-curtain dividers. A faded cradle roll hung on the front wall alongside the board that announced hymns and church and Sunday school attendance, even if the figures were an embarrassment. A shelf of unused, time-worn books graced one small corner and worn hymnals straggled in the pews.

I don't know what I learned in that setting, but I probably gained some Bible teaching—what my mind considered worth retaining. I won a small New Testament for writing a life of the apostle Peter in grade six.

Many Sundays Mother and Dad attended the Russian Baptist church seven miles out of town. Sometimes the service was held in our home during the winter. If we came home too early from the United Church Sunday school, we children waited quietly in the kitchen, snitching bits of food intended for our noon meal.

Sunday was a lazy day. We read, played games, worked at crafts. Dad relaxed in the rocking chair. In the evening we listened to a nostalgic family program that began with canaries twittering to music. Sometimes, as I grew older, I could be persuaded to go to church in the evening to represent the family. But generally the ecclesiastical institutions didn't intrude into our lives the way they sometimes do today. We liked it that way.

I think often, with remorse, of how I pushed and prodded my own children to go to church, to midweek, to youth groups, when they would rather have stayed at home. Or of how church attendance has sometimes been a compulsion for me. In my memories of growing up Christian, the church was there but didn't dominate.

In the United Church, an amalgam of Methodists, Presbyterians, and Anglicans, I can pick out people—the Sunday school superintendent, the choir leader, Sunday school teachers, lay members—who showed their calm determination to be the church no matter how few people attended, or how much or little leadership the pastor provided. Sometimes there was no pastor.

I sensed little judgment of one another's standing before Christ. All were sinners on a journey, not like across the river, where you were either "saved" or "going to hell" according to certain criteria, many of which had to do with observing certain *do's* and *don'ts*. In those churches you were in or out, with no category in between.

I grew up with a confusion of theologies. Across the river I encountered serious and forthright evangelicalism with its focus on crisis conversion, missions, evangelism and witnessing, and eschatology. On this home side, I experienced the weekly struggle to keep the lamp of faith burning in the church. We children knew subconsciously that we belonged on the other side by birth and religious background. But, because of some strange quirk of circumstances, we had landed among the unsaved, where we were "evangelized" along with the "heathen" by the other-side people we thought we belonged to.

I think of my childhood years as a time when I desperately wanted to be grown-up, to join the adult world, to get into the next stage. I dreamed about it, about getting married, about having children. A knight in shining armor would ride by my gate on a white horse and sweep me off my feet. But my problem was that I neglected to keep dreaming about what would come after that, and then after that, especially not about what life would be like when I was fifty or sixty, and God forbid, eighty or ninety.

Now I am there. As I think about growing up Christian, I think also about what it means to grow old(er) Christian.

The resemblances and differences between an older adult and a teenager are uncanny. Both are going through comparable traumatic experiences. Both are going through an identity crisis: What shall I be when I grow up? Who am I now that I don't have a career?

Old and young identify closely with the physical body and its changes—the young with developing strength and shape, the old with losing strength and loss of shape.

Large numbers in both groups may be using drugs of some kind—the one street drugs, the other prescription and over-the-counter drugs.

A sixteen-year-old is aspiring to acquire a driver's license. An eighty-year-old is thinking of turning it in.

Teenagers like their sofas overstuffed and roomy or else they head for the floor. Older adults look for a firm chair because they know a soft couch spells disaster. They may sit in it for eternity.

Both make travel a way of life—the one to games, retreats, lock-ins, band tours, field trips; the other on tour buses, recreational vehicles, and airplanes to see the world.

Both are thinking of changing housing. The young ones are off to college dormitories. The older ones head to retirement centers and nursing homes.

Both are looking for a way to steady their faith. One

group is growing up. The other is thought of as probably finished with growth—treading water.

Yet both need role models. We hear often that youth will be the future of the church but forget that older adults *are* the church, not *were*. Their example shows young people how to be that church.

Both are groups of people you do something for, rather than with. Yet older adults are the best ones to teach the young that Christianity works. If it doesn't carry the older adult through to the doorstep of eternity, why preach faith to the young?

When I was young we didn't talk a great deal about growing up. It was just taken for granted that you would. Now growing older is a taboo subject in some circles except to joke about. I found that during my fifties and sixties, I and my peers were hesitant to discuss our aging as openly as football scores and good restaurants, other than to rage, "It's going to be tough to get old."

We were never encouraged to talk about our deepest feelings when we were teenagers and don't know how to now. Thirty years ago who lived to be eighty and ninety? It becomes clearer to me that I am writing this book now because I believe that the discomfort I am experiencing is not unusual, just not openly discussed. I want to talk about my aging, and I am looking for other talkers.

People are expected to grow old alone emotionally without much support, even though they live in communities of the old (and I dare to use the dread taboo word "old"), because we see old age as something akin to the bubonic plague. The plague wiped out half the population of Europe during the Middle Ages; old age takes everyone who reaches that time of life.

Deeper feelings surface when I hear some of the early

and late retirees whisper, "Am I of use to anyone or anything? Am I needed? Even the congregation doesn't expect much of me at this point except to be grateful for small mercies and to bring finger food to socials."

I try to pin down elusive feelings about such words. The speakers voice fear of growing older because they don't know exactly when they will be old and what will be expected of them. They fear they may experience the ungainliness of a teenager about an adult situation. In North American society, old age is a time without a future. The elderly lose their role when they enter retirement but don't gain a new one. Being known as a retiree works for a while, but what are you after you have finished being a retiree?

I recall the morning I walked down the long hall of the educational wing to join the next older class. My own class had disbanded because many members had moved out of town. I felt like a high school student entering a college class. I would be identifying with the "old." A few people in this large class were at least seventy-five to eighty. I was only sixty-five. I was anxious. I didn't want to identify with this group. Yet unless I did, I would remain on the outer edge of the outer fringe of the church, like a teenager who never makes it to the center of the youth group. On the other hand, I knew older adults are the church and their modeling of Christian faith shows whether it has validity.

Another tough question older adults face is what difference being older makes to a person's inner wealth and to the spiritual resources of a congregation. The pastor across the table from me at a conference said, "Our congregation has only older people. It has no future." Her words said that to be an old Christian meant to be a dud. If I saw pastors vying for the job of ministering to congregations with half or more of their membership being mature, experienced, disciplined older adults, I'd know there was gold ahead instead of only white, blue, and yellow gray hair.

Those of us looking at old age from this side worry about retirement benefits from pensions and social security. But shouldn't we be more concerned about our source of spiritual strength? Where does it lie? What sustains the inner life?

So, as I think about growing old(er) Christian, I list my supports. Instead of Mother reading a Bible story, I take time for reflection and meditation after breakfast.

Congregating with the saints is more important now than it was then when I went as the token Funk to attend evening services as a child. The prophet Joel wrote that on the day of the Lord, the old men would dream dreams. I am strengthened when I see older persons remain strong members of the Christian body and hear them voice their dreams about the church of Jesus Christ.

I grow strong when I hear older adults speak the benediction at a service. Small thing, I know. Maybe I'm nostalgic for that comforting feeling I had in the little rural church we attended when I was a child, when one of the older, respected men in the congregation came forward at the end to bless the congregation. He knew what most of the farming families faced in the week to come. He was one of them.

I feel encouraged when I see older adults invited to join the visitation pastor in calling, not just on older adults, but also on younger families.

I feel encouraged when I see grandparents bless grandchildren at a dedication or baptism and see them stand up with new grandchildren to show solidarity.

I gain new strength when I see intergenerational activities or classes, with possibly a mentoring program of the young by the elderly, in which young and old get to know one another's joys and struggles more intimately.

Association with the older generation gives the younger generation practice in the art of living and dying. Life should not be a disjointed affair with each generation living isolated from the next, like sausage links. Life is a flowing stream. As one child marries and has children, at the other end of life the grandparents are letting go and moving on into the life beyond this one. God's grace and mercy is a part of all.

I am filled with joy when I hear the elderly share their stories and their gifts in a celebrative way. At my first older adult retreat, the group, totaling about one hundred people, enjoyed twenty-four hours of devotionals extremely well presented, stories that kept us riveted to our seats though we'd missed our naptime, and entertainment that rivaled Jay Leno.

Older adults are the strength of the church in terms of attendance as well as moral and financial support. They're the ones who go steady with the church. They're not likely to change affiliation when the church program no longer meets their needs.

I will feel even more encouraged when I hear more often how my elders confronted their own aging. It may be difficult for them to talk about something that has been buried deep inside, but I want the young to hear. And I want to hear.

My conclusion is that growing older Christian is not much different than growing up Christian. It's a matter of models and support. Mother and Dad were my models growing up. Older adults are my models now. I can be a model to younger men and women.

6

The curriculum is changing

Those who cannot change their minds cannot change anything. —George Bernard Shaw

I was teaching the short story "The Nose," by the Russian writer Gogol, in a college literature class. In it one of the characters, a barber, begins his day with a breakfast of bread, onions, and salt.

Bread, onions, and salt? "Who eats such a breakfast?" asked a student. I explained that during the Depression, I could remember people eating bread with anything that might give it flavor. Radish, cucumber, or tomato sandwiches were common. Meat sandwiches were rare. Lard or syrup sandwiches were not unheard of. Bread and onions sounded possible to me.

The student was reading the nineteenth-century story from his perspective of the twentieth century—onions and bread need a hamburger, mustard, ketchup, and some cheese in between. He and Gogol were working from two frames of reference.

Another two incidents. One involves a stand-up discussion in which three women my age, all of whom had been children during the 1930s, discussed their concern about the waste of food in their own children's homes. Platefuls of food were being dumped because it wasn't quite to the grandchild's liking.

The other incident was a casual discussion at lunch about the large quantity of food being served us at a regular meeting of older adults. Huge helpings of everything filled our plates, even though we are usually the ones who ask for a "senior plate." Someone mentioned an older woman who never left home without a Ziploc bag in her purse and another the man who went from table to table at such luncheons, advising, "Take home all leftovers— they'll just be trashed."

Were these people sitting at my table poor? Not at all. Were they greedy? I don't think so. I looked at the monster brownie on the dessert plate before me, cut off a corner to eat, and wrapped the rest in a napkin to take home. My neighbor did likewise. It just didn't make sense to have it thrown out because we couldn't eat it all. We had grown up with a different frame of reference and were acting accordingly, even if manners dictated otherwise.

People live by what they have been taught to believe is necessary and important. We then accept new facts and new experiences only if they fit our frame of reference or worldview. Changes comes with difficulty. But sometimes a paradigm shift—a change in worldviews—moves through society. Then such people must change their thinking also or be left sitting on the sidelines. Some see the shift away from ketchup to salsa and picante sauce as a paradigm shift, but I'm not quite convinced.

The industrial revolution was a major shift in people's thinking, as was the more recent shift to a high-tech information age, with the avalanche of information coming at us daily in many forms. Sometimes I think I am close to drowning in paper. If I don't act defensively, the flood overwhelms me. My first reaction to the daily mail is to discard the junk mail without opening it. Others are drowning in the information available on the computer Internet.

These paradigm shifts sometimes take us by surprise. Other times they creep up. I remember that, at the beginning of this revolution (not so long ago), I bought a reel-to-reel tape recorder despite the salesman's advice that this would soon become obsolete equipment. I couldn't shift that fast, I told myself. What if the electronic stuff didn't last? I'd have wasted my hard-earned money. My tape recorder has rested in a cupboard corner now almost since the month I bought it. I wasn't ready for the electronic revolution. Nor am I ready for super-computer systems with modems and much, much more.

When Jesus taught the people, he was aiming for a paradigm shift, a change in people's way of looking at life. He wanted to cut people loose from their foundations in the Law, not just to add bits of information for them to stuff into holes in their current worldview. He was saying to the crowds before him, "Here's a brand-new way of looking at life—a way of forgiveness and grace and love. But it means you'll have to let go of the Law."

For the Jews, that meant a complete shake-up in their thinking. And letting go of traditional thinking is one of the most difficult things to do. The religious leaders of his time couldn't let go; they had too much invested in the way things had always been done.

It's not unusual for members of one congregation to live unknowingly in two theological worlds, the one group adhering to a traditional conservative way of looking at the

Scriptures, the other ready to check out new paths of thought. Then they wonder why they are shouting at one another but not getting through.

New academic scholarship and archaeological findings about the Bible and about human behavior have carried one group along into acceptance of new thinking. The others are still deeply rooted in teaching they have accepted with comfort for decades. For example, one group may accept the Bible as a system of hierarchies, or a chain of command, in which God, Christ, angels, men, women, children, government and church leaders all find their precise pecking order. Any other view of the Bible doesn't make sense to them.

Another group may read the Bible from the frame of reference that at various times in biblical history God broke through to humanity, reestablishing and reinforcing, not hierarchies, but equality among humankind. To return to a hierarchical view seems like a return to the Dark Ages.

Some people, including older adults, pride themselves on being the only ones who still cling to God's truth. They show great resistance to change. They operate defensively and alienatingly. An older adult in an adult Bible class insists the King James version is the one to use. "They don't come any better," he argues. I wonder what he thought of the idea offered by another student that Priscilla, and not Timothy, as the King James suggests, may have been the author of the book of Hebrews? "Hebrews according to Prissie." Too horrible even to think about. Some older adults are open to considering new approaches, sometimes more so than middle-aged people. But others become more conservative as their bewilderment and fear of change increases.

Each day I grow older, I tell myself that if I want to survive I've got to keep sorting and sifting how what I believe relates to my daily life because that's where the biggest changes are taking place. My mother experienced tremendous changes from the simple rural life in the Russian steppes to a high-rise senior citizen center in a large metropolis. "Work out your salvation with fear and trembling," wrote the apostle Paul to the Philippian church. Mother did just that.

At times I was amazed at how easily she adapted with grace and compassion to what was going on around her and even to the modern lifestyles of family members. She didn't always understand what was happening, but she tried. If she could change, why should we of my generation who have experienced the Depression always respond as if the essence of that time still flows through our veins?

Like most people, I usually have reasons for responding as I do. Sometimes the basis for that reason is well supported with facts and organized in my mind; other times it's fuzzy. But I am bullheaded enough to believe that if I sort through the jumble, it will make sense. My life and behavior are rooted in my worldview gleaned from a lifetime of experience, thinking, and study.

But I worry about my blind spots. Can an older adult change? Should an older adult change? Psychologists suggest that for in the first half of life our goals are mostly personal and social—finding a vocation and partner, figuring out one's contribution to society, establishing financial security. When one has come to some understanding of this part of one's existence, and as one realizes humans are actually mortal (friends, parents, even children die), there is a change to seeking wisdom rather than power, writes Carl Jung.

Robertson Davies adds that this change to seeking wisdom does not make one an old man or an old woman. "What will make [the older adult] an old person is a frightened clinging to the values of the first half of life. The values that are proper and all-absorbing during the first half of life will not sustain a [person] during the second half" ("The Writer's Conscience," *Saturday Review*, March 18, 1978). He writes about the "shriveled Peter Pans" who dare not be their age. Outlook on life should match position in life.

I see Davies as meaning that, as I grow older, I may need to redefine what it means to be a contributing adult. I may need to change my script and move from one way of thinking that I have held dear for decades to another that takes into consideration changes in culture.

And that will take humility, faith, and grace, because arrogance plagues any group that believes it guards the sole truth. In some church settings, I ache when speakers and writers belittle anyone who can't agree with them that the Bible teaches only one view of women's roles—they are to be silent and submissive and know their place. I tell myself not to do the same with them—not to ridicule, belittle, and demean their "safe" position. They have reasons for what they believe.

We tend to forget that sometimes what we consider the absolute truth of the Word of God is but a thick slice of our particular culture thinly frosted by a few Scripture verses. Instead of letting the Word speak to us, we read our cultural prejudices into the issue, then promote that as God's truth. It is possible to take a few verses of Scripture and turn them into a doctrine that leads thousands astray, even though the entire thrust of the rest of the Bible may speak against such an unbalanced interpretation. Every once in a while, we need someone with courage to take a hard look at what is happening and then say to the rest of us, "You are promoting culture, not God's truth."

But what will help me to rethink and to reaffirm what I believe as an older adult? One morning the voice at the other end of the line asked if I was free to speak to a group of women on a certain date. "Sure," I said, "but what kind of an audience will I have?"

Somewhat hesitantly the voice said, "Mostly between fifty and seventy." She really meant between sixty and eighty. I felt she was telling me that this organization had grown old with its members and not attracted new ones. Younger women were going in a different direction.

Why apologize? I asked myself. Those who attend many church events are mostly mature adults. They have made their main contribution to life but are loyal to the church and need inspirational gatherings.

But what do you say to an audience or a congregation in which most of those present are not blatant backsliders but the faithful over-sixty bunch? Do you keep evangelizing them? Do you keep "reviving" them by encouraging them to keep at the Christian disciplines of prayer, Bible study, and good works? I admit I sometimes grow weary of Bible study after Bible study in which we keep going over the "fundamentals of the faith," something the writer of Hebrews cautioned against.

I thought of this phone call when I attended a youth meeting several years ago at which popular speaker Tony Campolo challenged young people to sacrifice their lives for God's kingdom. Campolo's unique blend of humor, showmanship, oratory, theology, empathy for outsiders, and the ability to turn a sermon into an art form made an hour and a half seem as if the tape was moving fast forward. Campolo told young people, Change your lifestyle and location if need be, and devote your lives to the Lord.

What about the others—the AARP group? What sacrifice should be expected of them? Geographic relocation is not likely when you're deeply rooted in a satisfying vocation and in the midst of family joys and concerns. Or when older adults have joined the RV society and roam the country, having no fixed place of abode other than a house on wheels. They want geographic relocation on their terms.

Campolo had an answer the second night of his services. Older Christians may not be able to move to Philadelphia or other cities to work with inner city youth, except for several weeks or months at a time. But they have a task also, maybe even a harder one—to give up their firmly held attitude that their theology is always right.

I heard him saying that for the church to be the church, older Christians will have to revise their "oral law" toward fringe people, little people, unlovable people—attitudes some have cherished and nurtured for nearly a lifetime, yet consider "Christian" because they seem so normal.

To change one's thinking is tough. It takes a conversion, a *metanoia*, a turning around. Our theology has taught us to hate sin. Somehow hating the sinner becomes part of that theology. Then to change our thinking about these unclean people seems to mean we're changing what we believe, even changing the Bible.

I don't like change, any kind of change. I don't like it when my routine changes, as when I forget to set the alarm and sleep in. Getting up late upsets me because I don't get started on the new day the usual way. I may have to cut out a cup of coffee or reading the paper. I don't like it when people do things differently. To my own dismay, I mutter bad words to myself when I have to look for the paper down the walk instead of finding it in its usual place in front of the screen door. "Must be a new paper carrier . . . what an irresponsible person . . . and no plastic wrapper."

We grow when we deliberately examine our own belief system brought together after years of living, listening, and watching others. I think back to the theology I heard most about as a young adult. Matthew 28:19 was the most important text in the Bible: "Go ye into all the world and preach the gospel." Conversion, mission, and evangelism were the warp and woof of the religious fabric of these people. I heard that the cross meant pray, give, GO. Growing church budgets for missions was clear evidence of God's blessing. For a mother to have a child go into missionary service was to know God's highest blessing on her family.

This emphasis on evangelism and missions had another side to the coin. "Don't do anything that God might misread as an attempt to earn divine favor." You never spoke about conversion and good works in the same breath, for to do so might taint the former. People showed faith only when they were openly pious.

Furthermore, when I was young, activism in any form was a bad word. Activism meant you were perilously close to the edge of damnation and possibly false teachings. The only activism permitted was witnessing in some form through word of mouth, maybe going door-to-door asking people if they were Christians.

Salvation in my growing-up years was considered an individual affair between the person and God, not becoming a member of a community of faith. God works, but only in one heart at a time, never in structures and systems, not even through the body of Christ as a whole.

Widespread prejudice against other races, classes, and sexes was the result of an individual's warped thinking, never societal patterns of sin.

Then as I grew older, I became aware of a radical redefinition of the meaning of the cross. This new definition asked me, as a Christian, to make room for minorities and women, maybe even as leaders in the church. God expected me to think through people's needs for intimacy, justice, and truth-speaking; to work my way through questions of pluralism, human sexuality, and eschatology. But that would mean diving into these subjects headfirst with the intent of discovering the truth as it applied to me today, not just several thousand years ago.

Another question that edged up close to the one I have just mentioned and waited patiently for an answer was the unchangeableness of God. In time of much change, caused by war, depression, migration, illness, and natural disaster, an unchangeable God is necessary. "Abide with me, Oh, thou that changest not, abide with me," was a favorite hymn when year after year the fields remained dry and parched.

But that teaching about the immutability of God sometimes became a teaching that God was set against change of any kind. To change one's thinking about God was to turn one's back on the Redeemer, forgetting that a changeless God looks for change in us.

The God I believed in when I was young always worked miraculously, overnight. Conversion was a crisis event and could be traced to a time, a day, a place, a verse of Scripture. It was preceded by a period of intense conviction about sin. Then came the light-bringing moment, sometimes brought about by reading a scrap of the Bible. Bad habits like smoking, drinking, gambling, and so forth evaporated with the morning mist. God was doing a new thing. The emphasis was on human wickedness and human inability to change self—only God could do that. The believer's only task was to pray.

Is it any wonder I am perplexed by Twelve-step programs and support groups aimed at helping people cope with their addictions over time, sometimes years? What happened to yesterday's miracles? A large share of Christian literature today is how-to literature—how to cope with life's blows through counseling over months, even years. Where is the instantaneous miraculous power of God? Is God's hand shortened? Has God changed? Do people no longer make spiritual transactions with God and experience God's grace and power?

Another matter. Success in those days was important. It seemed right and important to keep moving up the economic and social ladder. Christianity conferred blessings rather than demanded costs. In small rural communities, peace and harmony were always more important than justice, so children grew up to the familiar refrain, "What will the people say?" and struggled for years to find their own voice.

The glue that held small communities together was responsibility for one another. You misbehaved in the sandlot and your parents knew about it before you got home. In a modern urban community, where people don't know one another, who worries about what the people will think? But sometimes, in the quiet of my heart, I betray myself and my need to free myself from the burden of satisfying others. I wonder if it wouldn't be better if at least sometimes people worried about what the neighbor thought about them.

Yes, we always learn our theology well. And to change

in any respect seems a small rebellion. Yet respectful dissent, even doubt or change in theology, should be viewed, not as a disloyal challenge to the Bible, but as a necessary part of our growth in understanding. As an older adult, I feel less compelled to claim certainty for the church's teachings. As I watch "Christian" television programs with their glitz and glamor, I ask myself, If that is the church, where is the Christ who, like the scapegoat, went beyond the camp bearing our reproach?

To grow older is to change. Here are changes in theology I have had to make over the years. And I expect to make more. The change was never a sudden event, but usually evolved with study, prayer, and openness. And much pain.

- The Holy Spirit has a gift for service for every believer, including me.
- Interdenominational cooperation is not only valuable but necessary in a shrinking world.
- Two people can hold to different interpretations of the same passage of Scripture yet be children of God.
- The best Bible translations are those done by a community of scholars, not an individual, using the best tools of linguistic, historical, and archaeological research. I've let go of the King James Version, although I love the stately phraseology and choice of words.
- Older adults need spiritual teaching directed specifically to them, just as young adults need teaching directed specifically to them.
- I no longer believe that evil resides only in individuals. Like goodness and truth, it resides also in social systems developed by human beings. When Jesus spoke against the Pharisees, he was speaking against the evil in the religious structures and systems of his day, not simply

against individuals. But when he spoke to the woman at the well, he was addressing her as an individual. Jesus worked both fronts.

- It is difficult to be a Christian in isolation from the body of Christ. The church of Jesus Christ, imperfect as it may be, holds the key to personal growth and service.

I could add many others, especially as they relate to human sexuality and the age-old question of good people suffering when God has power to change their situations. That is the beginning of another book.

So what is our task as older adults? It is harder, I think, than what Campolo asked of the youth. We have to lead in love, to close the gap, both giving love and being courageous enough to speak the truth in love.

7

Older adult spirituality

Spiritual rose bushes are not like natural rose bushes; with these latter the thorns remain but the roses pass, with the former the thorns pass and the roses remain. —St. Francis de Sales

At the beginning of the Christian life, we start off with a passion for getting everyone into the kingdom of God as fast as possible. And we are sure we can do it. Evangelist Billy Graham said in a television interview that as a young man he believed firmly it was possible to evangelize the world in a lifetime—*his* lifetime. As zealous young Christians, we allow ourselves to believe that God is tottering on his last legs and won't get the job done without us. "He has no hands but our hands, no feet but our feet, to bring the message to others" is the hymn our youth groups sang several decades ago—and believed. We—or no one.

We became impatient with Christians who slogged along apathetically. Why didn't they get on with it? The heathen were dying without Christ, we had the word of truth, let's move! When I first made a serious commitment to Christ at age nineteen, I read the Bible with the hunger of someone who had been denied food for a month. And I had no time for less serious stuff. I had found the meaning of life and didn't expect to change my vision of Christ's kingdom (shaped by my Scofield Bible) in the future.

Admittedly, I and my young friends attending Bible college in the middle 1940s had more zeal than wisdom. One older friend, on her way to the mission field, knew she had to prove herself to her mission board. With me in tow, she headed downtown, where people strolled the streets on a Saturday evening, to confront one unsuspecting person after another with the need to repent and confess Christ as Savior. She literally grabbed them by the lapels and forced them to listen to her.

Another friend, whose parents had belonged to the same school of thought about personal evangelism, tells of spending Sunday afternoons throwing "bomb" tracts. He and his father wrapped religious tracts in tubes of red cellophane. Then, as his father drove slowly alongside the sidewalk, the son directed these "bombs" to land at the feet of a surprised pedestrian. His father was convinced God would use any committed effort. And God probably did in ways we know nothing about.

When we first encounter the Word of God as young adults, we approach it with a childlike naivete, an uncritical belief, devouring the Bible like a famished refugee. Belief about anything comes easy if promoted by a convincing messenger. Acting on that belief is important.

But later, after more reflection and experience with the hard spots of life and the frailties of the community of believers, some Christians slowly distance themselves from the Word and the working of the Spirit. As they look more critically at the text and the preaching and teaching about it, they wonder why what they hear and read doesn't always match their life experiences. The awareness that what they hear preached contains beautiful sweeping generalities unsubstantiated by the Word may come suddenly, more often gradually. Contrary to what they were taught, God is not a mail-order catalog.

Some people lose their faith at this stage, or push it to the back of their minds. To them it seems impossible to harmonize much-repeated theological propositions with the realities of life. This second stage of spiritual development is sometimes one of disillusionment, of loss, of grief at the need to relinquish that early passion for truth. Sometimes there is even bitterness at having spent too much time with something that didn't pan out. More often the reaction is a slow leeching of faith, evidenced by a gradual withdrawal from the community of faith.

Some people never move beyond this stage of silent confusion. Instead, to relieve their discomfort, they synthesize their values, information, and thinking into a neat little package.

As a new Christian, I had written in the back of my Scofield Bible a statement to that there was a condition to every promise of God. If I did my part, God would do his. I recall that at the time I thought I had discovered the formula for Christian success. (And how some of us are addicted to reducing everything to lists, to formulas, to propositions!) Now all I had to do was figure out how to meet those conditions, and I could hold God to his promise. I was in control. I was on my way.

But I learned that life doesn't work this way, especially when I was introduced to suffering, evil, and injustice. "Life isn't fair," said my father often as we children were growing up. He knew from experience that sometimes unusual circumstances or natural events, such as storm, rain, drought, manipulated people like the ingredients of a milkshake in a blender. War and depression forced many people into boxes not of their own choosing. Life didn't reward you according to the effort you put into it or how good you were, he warned me.

But I knew better. I believed in a fair world. If I committed my whole life to the work of the Lord, surely God would supply my needs in abundance. Obedience in, rewards out—just like a computer, just like the early Israelites had believed. But then for a time I wandered with these Israelites in the wilderness, lamenting God's seeming absence and wondering why God had deserted me.

"Up to thirty years of age life is full of promise; after that, life holds out no more promise; it holds out the test as to whether we are going to live up to what we saw in the vision," writes Oswald Chambers in *God's Workmanship.* It's a question of "hanging on" in the dark to what we saw in the light.

For those who hold onto faith during the valley experiences, there is another stage in spiritual development which brings a new possibility for spiritual growth and joy. The believer's relationship to God is restored, with or without evidence of God's activities on our behalf. Now we affirm joyfully God's unconditional love and place in our lives. We regain courage to deal with unpleasant or ambiguous realities of life and accept life's injustices because we are on a journey with God—and toward God.

In this stage, wonder for the power of the Word is restored. The Bible is again God's Word but at a level deepened by confronting personal struggles and doubts.

I write these things because I am convinced many older Christians are in this third stage of spiritual development. They have lived through numerous changes, successes, and defeats in their religious life. But they hung on.

They may have fallen, but they did not stay down when life blasted them with heavy blows. They relinquished the luxury of despair for the joy in the Lord. As Robert Cole points out, this grace is not handed out to people "who are smiling all the time and go to church every Sunday." True faith does not become mired in obstacles. It moves through the darkness of perplexity to that stage when life becomes daily grace.

I think about the many older adults I know. Even as the Egyptians experienced good and bad years, these stalwarts in the faith knew good years followed by difficult years, in which many of them witnessed the suffering of thousands through war, drought, famine, flood, mass hunger, and homelessness.

In their lifetime they attended dozens of annual revival meetings, once considered the complete and best answer to evangelism. They now find these highly-cherished events have become a memory—sometimes a poignant loss, sometimes a bitter recollection about having been manipulated into decisions.

They have witnessed many changes in people's values. What they once understood as being the highest calling in life, becoming a missionary, has lost its glamor in today's church culture. These older adults have watched the communal movement of the 1970s, which seemed to herald a new age for the church, slump into organizationalism and harden along institutional lines.

I think the church at times must seem very human to these older adults. With large and growing professional staffs, the local church looks like any other secular organization but with a different product to sell. I've heard older adults compare the church with business enterprises. Both enjoy excellent management, topline computing systems, and slick marketing skills. But the discussion, though well-seasoned with grace, is sometimes followed by the harrowing question: Where is the mystery of the divine corporate life of which Paul wrote to the Ephesian church and which once motivated them to pray, to give, and to go? Even their familiar language about God and their hymns which told "the old story" no longer have a place in modern worship settings.

These people from another era know what it is like to see favorite teachings, like premillenialism, fall into disfavor. To observe the struggle between creationism and evolution. And to watch highly respected leaders, once the symbols of religious authority, tumble. Everything in the new Christian life today has to be "fun" and "exciting." The success of a Sunday school class lies in whether the video was entertaining, not whether it moved someone to live out the gospel as a more dedicated disciple.

Sunday morning services have become variety shows. The services seem taken over by clapping and drums; they have little sense of the sacred or of God's transcendence in a spiritual sense, as older adults once knew it. Some tremble as they watch trust in psychology and counseling and the language of psychobabble replace a simple faith in the power of the Lamb to save sinners and give power over sin. What happened to the reality that forgiveness of sin, before God or before humankind, is a spiritual cleansing, not just a coping skill? And whatever happened to sin?

Yet these older adults acknowledge Christ's presence and strength with them, not to assure them wealth and happiness, but to see them through each day's struggles. They are convinced of the need to keep witnessing to Christ's righteousness even if evil seems to be in control—not because of the promise of great success, but because God asks for obedience.

Vibrant older Christians have their faith intact because they know there is nothing else to hang onto that provides a steady anchor. Money, estate, position, prestige, and reputation don't provide that security. Divorce, illness, homosexuality, abuse, and similar matters affect their families as much as anyone else's. I know of some older adults who grieved greatly because of marriage breakups in their family, but the tragedy didn't affect their faith in God. With Peter, they kept saying, "Lord, to whom shall we go? You alone have the words of eternal life."

They continue to find faith meaningful even when younger people look at their circumscribed lives and surmise they couldn't possibly have a significant relationship with God because nothing's happening. Their daily moments have significance because they trust God. And these moments of trust join to form a pattern of meaning. I have seen this joy in life in numbers of older adults, living alone, with limited contacts. A few probing comments soon bring out evidence of a faith that perseveres.

They know from experience that good people are not immune to suffering. They cannot give precise answers to the reasons for injustice in this world. As Daniel J. Simundsen writes in *Hope for all Seasons*, they "have not received their share of the world's resources, not been protected from anger, not received justice from this world, and have not been supported by loving communities." But they continue to have faith. They have been blessed with a serene sense of the God-givenness of life.

The words they say are not much different than those they uttered about God and the Word at the beginning of their faith pilgrimage. But the basis for them is deeper, more secure. And they continue to volunteer and serve the church as they are able. They know God will evaluate their contributions in the light of their opportunities. They leave this report-card work to God.

A good word to describe this third stage Is *Gelassenheit*—which means a simple yielding to God without frills. Such an attitude acknowledges that we are in God's hands and that God is on our side, no matter what happens. We worship God, not for what we can get out of him, but because God is God. Those who handle old age best are those who "maintain options, who control at least their inner world, as they become frailer," writes gerontologist Gerald A. Larue. I see their deliberate yielding to God as a way to control the ups and downs of life. They allow God to remain sovereign.

This spirit of *Gelassenheit* is most evident among older people who have found that God takes them through the difficult days and perplexing new ways of doing church to a surer place that rises above the trivia. They have set their vision on a hope that lies beyond this life. They know that everyone must do their own believing. And praying. And serving. And so, if their eyesight is bad, they write their prayer lists in large print on wrapping paper. Because prayer is important. That and waiting in hope for the promise of their Redeemer.

A clear, cherished image I carry with me is the memory of the high-pitched voice of the old woman living in the room next to mine in a boarding house when I was about twenty. Every evening before she went to bed, she cried to her God. My roommate and I could count on it. We stopped our chatter and listened with awe. With such people in the Christian community, the church will survive, for they serve as models of the next generation.

Theologian Jacques Ellul has been helpful to me more

than once. He writes in *Living Faith* that in our age we have come to see faith as a tool, an instrument, to order our worlds, to solve our problems, to make life easier and better for ourselves. Faith then becomes the means toward an end, our end. That's presumption. That's daring ourselves to walk the ridgepole, forcing God to act on our behalf.

Ellul's thesis is that we must relearn what faith is all about, that it is a state of trust in God and God's Word. We believe in God for "nothing." Our faith witnesses to the reality of the One who said, "I am." Our faith also moves us to action to reveal the reality of our God to others.

But this strong faith, which I see most often in older Christians, does not seem to be an image of power and strength because we live in a time when vigor, personality, and aggressiveness are most valued. Evelyn Eaton Whitehead and James D. Whitehead write in *Christian Life Patterns* that the elderly will not be included in the ongoingness of life unless they are conceived as "powerful and graced with strengths which are of value" to society.

If people's images of older people are mostly negative —dependence, weakness, and suffering—they will shape the elderly into that image. And turn all elderly into needy persons. And this kind of vulnerable faith is disposable in a society that wants faith to be "exciting" and dramatic.

Yet people with a spirit of yieldedness, or *Gelassenheit,* are the only ones who can teach the young that Christianity works and that prayer is the key to life lived with God.

I remind myself that spiritual maturity or *Gelassenheit,* words that are not quite synonyms, is seldom reached at a young age, even though spiritually precocious youngsters are often shoved into positions beyond them. The great saints of the faith only seemed to perfect themselves after they were fifty and older. As one person said, a young minister may be brilliant, but an older man is more often wise.

The young show great zeal and spirit, often rushing tempestuously forward in support of a great cause and convinced they have the whole answer. We need such enthusiasm. But we also need the ones who see the world steady and whole despite experiences of war, family breakup, job loss, illness, death, and serious disputes. We need the ones who can match zeal with inner stability.

While visiting another congregation, I picked up in the hall one of those prayer score sheets which had fallen out of some child's hands. On tabular paper on one side was room for listing dates and prayer requests. On the right-hand side was room for another date and the answer to the prayer. Before long will someone work out software strategies for keeping God in line through prayer? Would a prayer warrior of seventy or eighty use such a sheet? Or would such a person just keep praying, whether the answers showed up or not?

The stories older people tell are often about God's breakthroughs, those *kairos* moments in their lives that become clearer with each year. The events may have been ambiguous for a time, but the light of additional experience convinces the older adult that God is with him or her. So they speak of these experiences with boldness, convinced they have located the spokes in the wheel of God's grace.

One last point regarding older adult spirituality. Several years ago Quaker futurist Elise Boulding talked to a college conference about the importance of humans becoming, growing. Our society used to talk about what humans could become if they used all their faculties, she said. This is no longer true. Today conventional thinking is that what happens inside you is not my business. When choices need to be made, technology makes them rather than humans. Real development is what can be measured by machines.

To focus on humans becoming means to create a new vision of the task. It includes our intellect and our spirituality, including prayer and intuition, said Boulding—but also our fantasies, our imagination, our daydreams. People need to daydream about how things could be in our society. They need to recover an image of the future, of the possibility. Changes have come out of the imaginings or visions of people.

She advised all students entering college to spend the first week working on imaging the kind of world Jesus envisioned and how they would fit into it. What could they do in the present? What courses should they take to make the vision a reality? What skills should they learn?

I believe that dreaming, envisioning the future of church and society, is also the spiritual role of the freshman elder. Responsibility rests on those who have found signs of God's wisdom in their lives to speak out and to clarify to all, "I am not yet at the end of my journey. This is the way I envision God's plan for the church."

So at this point in my border crossing, I recognize that it is important to see this period in my life as a real crossing and to make no apology for stumbling in crossing it. In fact, I am thankful I began recording my journey. I write this book to dignify the confusion about my dreams, sometimes clear, sometimes without form.

I am no longer willing to accept superficial answers to difficult questions about life and aging. I admit that I struggle with some questions of faith. Why doesn't faith empower people to turn from sin? Is the arm of the Lord

shortened and his ear closed? Why has counseling replaced faith and the church in meeting human need? How
can we contain the forces of evil? "The darkness deepens,
Lord, with me abide."

Where is family love in a world of homeless, neglected,
starving, unhealthy, abused children? Why are we reluctant to side with the poor? How can we remain so self-
serving in church life in the name of "nurturing" and yet
say we preach the gospel of the cross?

This crossing is a real test because of the alternatives. I
can subside into a blob that merely exists, and how tempt-
ing that sometimes is. I can become a windup toy that
plays itself out. Or I can move ahead more surely. So any
advice I offer here, I give myself.

When I started this book I didn't know how it would
end. I once refused a book contract for that reason. I didn't
have the resolution to my thesis in mind and wasn't willing to risk a manuscript. Even now I don't know where I
am headed. But I am ready to say that this book is a defense of myself, of all border crossers searching for a
stronger sense of security and self-respect and the right to
dream and to speak about their dreams. A border crossing
is not a test of faith but of identity.

Several years ago our family enjoyed the friendship of
a young Chinese student, newly arrived from what was
then known as Formosa. He addressed my husband, then
in his early forties, as "old man," much to my spouse's
amusement. To Larry, however, the term was one of great
respect and honor. So, "old man, old woman," no matter
how old you are, let's keep moving. The journey of a thousand miles begins with one step. Heads high, shoulders
back, we're on the move. Toward *Gelassenheit?* And to big-
ger dreams? Could be.

8

Growing old(er) in a win/lose culture

*Even though our outer nature is wasting away,
our inner nature is being renewed day by day.*
—2 Cor. 4:16, NRSV

Ours is a win/lose culture. We are encouraged to be winners, if not by our brains, then by luck. Some people regularly buy lottery tickets when they buy gas or groceries; it's part of their budget. Others faithfully enter mail sweepstakes, rationalizing that the only investment is the cost of a stamp. And who knows, they might win a few million dollars and live a life of ease forever after.

Our society has little room for anyone who fails in sports. Players and coaches who haven't become or produced winners are traded or dismissed for a better prospect. In the entertainment, business, or academic world, it's important to stay at the top. A C grade is no longer a gentleman's grade but a failing mark.

In the religious world, the win/lose mentality also holds. When I was younger, if you hadn't won many souls to Christ, you were a loser of the worst kind. You carried a heavy load of guilt each day. Today the win/lose mentality crops up in a different way. The church able to attract the most people, even if only in the process colloquially known as "rearranging the saints," is considered successful. That other congregations are losing their members as a result is not considered.

Is it any wonder, then, that in such a culture growing older is considered a losing proposition? Society has two images of aging: deterioration/loss and growth/wisdom. But the first image is the dominant one. Physically, the old are obvious losers. You lose your eyesight, hearing, and hair gradually, sometimes as young as age thirty. Then other little flaws show up one by one. One day it's a gray hair, then a few more wrinkles, then agility and an inability to remember names. After that you're racing downhill.

To spend time with a number of older adults means becoming aware of the growing frailty of the body. Sometimes their conversation can't get down to serious discussion until the slate has been cleared by mentioning everyone with health problems. The message is clear that the body is beginning to break down. It's a form of losing. But other losses join these—death of friends and family members, position, opportunities for activity, mobility, finances.

During the working years, it seems right and normal to keep climbing, to acquire more money, position, and power with each rung of the career ladder. Yet the more you pushed for success in the middle years, the harder withdrawal becomes when that career ends. The more your identity came from a successful career, position, or strong reputation, the harder it is to start climbing down the ladder.

The end of a career may bring with it a plummeting in self-esteem. Suddenly you realize you're in a battle for your dignity and life, both as an individual and as a member of an age group you'd rather not be in. So you turn to self-help books on aging to find ways to turn yourself into a winner once again. The answer usually has to do with self-esteem.

In some congregations, younger members mistakenly think that only what is done for families with children has lasting value. After all, children are the future church. Yet older adults are the present church. The presence of older adults should be a constant reminder to younger generations that they won't always be young. Death will come. Life will be over, at least on this earth, sometime.

What does God intend for the older adult? I've asked this question hundreds of times. I asked it again when, before her death, I sat beside the bedside of my ninety-eight-year-old mother in the hospital; she was physically helpless, all her peers were gone, and her cognitive abilities were diminishing. What liberates an older adult from the win/lose mentality when winning on society's terms isn't a possibility?

I see the submission of servanthood as the only answer. The essence of this servanthood is to become good at losing, at making room for others, especially the younger generation, to be the winners. This ability enables the elders to resist seeing this younger group as threats to their authority or ominous signs that they're being set aside.

But that raises another question. The older adult is possibly living alone on a limited income, with weakening physical strength. Is it possible for this person to choose the servant identity when deterioration/loss/submission is already a dominant image of aging?

Our society, one that upholds human rights above all

else, is notably ambivalent and even opposed to anything that smacks of giving up rights or power or sharing it with others. But having power isn't usually the older adult's problem. My mother had little noticeable power in the last years of her life. She was increasingly dependent on others. So how can I advocate submission to people already without power? Because submission is power.

Our strongest image of servanthood comes from the life of Jesus, a young teacher in his early thirties, especially in the account of his washing the disciples' feet. The story troubles me. I admit I don't know what a servant looks like today, especially when that servant is an older person living semi-isolated at home or in a nursing home.

As I read the story of Jesus washing the disciples' feet, I see men in flowing robes reclining on low couches in the room prepared for them—by some servant? Well, I would think so. If that is the case, what happened to that servant? Obviously there was one once, yet no servant appears in the doorway to perform the lowly but necessary task of washing the guests' feet. But a basin of water and a towel have been left in a corner of the room—a thoughtful if incomplete gesture.

This ancient rite of washing the guests' feet was both a ceremonial task and a practical need. The men were probably uncomfortable after walking the hot dusty streets in sandals, but they didn't know how to relieve their discomfort without a servant. Some of them possibly eyed the basin in the corner, but then they weren't servants, so they didn't touch it.

I compare their situation to my discomfort when I enter a home in winter and no one offers to take my coat. What am I do with it? Keep it on? Dump it on a chair? What about my boots? Do I remain in the hallway or walk on the rug with wet boots? Am I welcome? Am I supposed to leave?

Jesus, as host of the meal, took the basin and towel. Kneeling before each disciple, Jesus washed his feet, an act that made the disciples uncomfortable—maybe even feel guilty. Their respected teacher was doing a lowly servant's job, one they wouldn't stoop to.

In our contemporary society, which encourages each of us to stand up for our rights, we stumble at the word *servant*, the word I am suggesting should describe the older adult. Though we use a lot of servanthood language, most middle-class North American children have never seen an actual servant nor do they know what a servant's posture was in Bible times. In homes with modern plumbing, many have never seen a wash basin and towel used together. They know that when your feet are dirty, you get into the shower or tub—without help from the host.

I find that our images of servanthood in the Christian community are fuzzy, but those of power and authority are clear. The power role has a way of getting to us at any age in life. We all like to be recognized and stroked. I can list many words that cater to power—permit, let, command, dominate, rule, govern, allow, grant, concede, tolerate, suffer, sanction, insist, oblige, require, hold down, forbid, ban, prohibit, regulate, control, direct, restrain, master, elect, compel, restrict, interdict, manage—and I've just begun my list.

I can also list many kinds of authority figures without much thought—king, president, army commander, administrator, chief executive officer, anchor person, chair, director, and senior pastor. A lifetime of living with such power language ill prepares us to become good at the losing that accompanies aging.

My list of servant figures is harder to produce. It is difficult to find the image of a servant in an age of managers, administrators, and public relations persons with brief case, car phone, beeper and pager, chronological watch, answering service, fax machine, yellow legal pad, lap computer, and array of secretaries and clerks.

The very word *servant* resurrects racist images of bug-eyed black waiters in 1930s movies; maids with frills and caps, curtsying; Uriah Heap-type clerks; dumb blonde secretaries; and lowly peons in Eastern countries salaaming to the ground to show their subservience. Servanthood invokes thoughts of unequal pay, lack of recognition, and loss of freedom as the penalty for being powerless.

It has been a long time since I've seen a true servant. Just any hired employee doesn't fit the description. When I need work done in my house, I'm the one saying, "Yes, sir" and "No, sir" to the plumber or electrician, rather than the other way around. They aren't my servants. Nor am I theirs. We've simply made an agreement of payment for services rendered.

To discuss power is like talking about the contents of the neighbor's dirty laundry hamper. We know it's there sitting in some corner. But what's in it is the other person's business. Many older adults have moved through their middle years with a great deal of power. Their very presence evoked confidence. It came from financial status, education, sex, race, social position, personal achievement, or family background. And occasionally through election or appointment.

The paradox is that power is a prerequisite for true servanthood. Servanthood occurs when power rightfully achieved in any area is willingly yielded in the interests of others. The strength of servanthood is vulnerability, not impenetrable armor.

The true servant sits where people sit, thinks their thoughts, suffers their pain and their doubts, and becomes liable for their mistakes and failures. As soon as liability for another is qualified to any degree, servanthood is diminished. The true servant meets needs and affections. His or her main quality is devotion rather than efficiency, tradition, and propriety. A true servant has the power of healing, of tearing down walls, like the Chinese servant Lee in John Steinbeck's *East of Eden*.

Lee, long-term servant in the Trask family, experiences the brutality of prejudice against his race, but it does not embitter him. Over a period of years, he becomes the most influential person in the home, for he is in touch with all family members. A white friend asks him why he is contented as a servant. He replies, "It is a position of power, even of love. . . . a good servant can completely control his master, tell him what to think, how to act, whom to marry, when to divorce, reduce him to terror as a discipline, or distribute happiness to him."

Lee chooses to use his power for good. He deliberately gives up his own dreams to own his own bookstore when given the choice and returns to the Trask family as servant. Here he sees his values, goals, and influence sway the people he works for. Lee, as reconciler, brings the estranged family together.

I don't want to preach servanthood at a group of people—the aging—who can never choose to be anything but what they are—increasingly powerless in a win/lose society. To do so would be to push more powerlessness upon this group of older adults. Enforced subservience puts people in an adversary position. Servanthood then dictates, "Be satisfied in your role; don't aspire to use your full strength." No husband, for example, can force a wife to obey him; she can, however, willingly submit to him. Submission is a two-way street; it works both up and down.

Let me clarify my definition of a servant a little more. A servant is one who has a vision of the possibilities that can happen by the grace of God. The purpose of servanthood is to impart God's truth to another person in a relationship. The servant Lee becomes effective because of his vision of reconciliation between the embittered father and surviving son in the Trask family. His sole purpose for a time becomes bringing that about.

I see such willing servanthood in people who during the difficult thirties had to set aside dreams for themselves as professionals and leaders in church and society and accept another role in life, sometimes low-paying manual labor, because there was no money for education. Some of these achieved more influence in this role of submission than had they gone on to get degrees and amass fortunes. But unless they accepted their limitations with joy, their lives were daily bitterness.

So here is one of my first clues to older adult servanthood. Older adult servants at some point accept their lives as they are: "That's my life. That's the way it must be." They admit and submit to their mortality. They accept the givenness of their own lives and start dreaming in big measure for the next generation. In other words, they see with Christ's eyes the possibilities of what the Holy Spirit can do in the lives of young people and children. That's a true servant's task. The prophet Joel wrote about "old men dreaming dreams." When very old people dream, it is no longer for themselves but for others. And that requires submission and joy. When such people die, they leave behind a legacy of values that brings the younger generation through to the larger life.

End-stage servants continue to care for and pray for persons, nations, ideas, and institutions whose future they will not share. They continue loving the church as Christ's body. They love and mentor children and grandchildren, their own and others. Without a vision of possibilities for the next generation and opportunities to transmit that vision, older adults revert to the withdrawal/loss mentality. Unless the older adults envision and work toward a strong younger generation, they become nothing more than a group of aging individuals, each privately enjoying a relationship with Christ whose connections to this life end when they die.

But a dream, a vision, is not enough. As they are able, older adults also articulate their vision for the church. People with a well-articulated charismatic vision inspire other people. Singer Elvis Presley had a vision of helping people release their inhibitions, and our society has never been the same. Older adults must not keep silent.

Difficult assignment? Yes, especially in some modern congregations that are so closely age-graded that interaction between the generations is nearly impossible. Yet I believe that older adults with a servanthood mentality become aware of their generation's place and responsibility in the sequence of the generations. Isaac honored Abraham and Sarah, his parents, but he blessed Jacob and Esau, his sons. Servanthood means recognizing that ours is not the only generation, but that we are part of the river of life. Life starts, develops, slows down, and ends. But there is always another beginning. God's purpose for the older adult is to complete the life cycle, to bind the generations together, to hand over the faith.

My mother, shortly before she died, mentioned to me that she couldn't pray like she used to. She had prayed daily for children and grandchildren by name. My comfort to her was that that part of her lifework was done. She could let go and hand that task on to others.

A second clue to older adult servanthood has to do with choosing, something most crucial in the servant/disciple role. Jesus picked up a basin and towel and washed his disciples' feet to illustrate this matter of choice. He chose to be a servant. In Bible times a servant was a slave or hired person who had to work for another person. A servant had little choice. Servants, together with strangers, widows, and orphans, were grouped near the bottom of the social ladder. Anyone who could choose didn't seek membership in this social category.

My parents often explained to us children what it actually felt like to be a low-class servant in the Russian-Mennonite culture of South Russia, where the differences between rich and poor were marked. As a young woman, Mother worked on a large estate from early dawn until darkness decreed work must end. Sometimes, even though she was weary from hard work in the kitchen, she had to spend the evening crocheting doilies for the mistress of the home. Her total day belonged to her employer.

Her stories about her early life as an actual servant showed me that a servant is a person who knows the death of his or her own personal dreams and ambitions. They are shelved, perhaps indefinitely, in the interests of master or mistress, like those of the servant Lee. A servant is a person who moves in the rhythms and patterns of the one in charge. Someone else decides when it is time to get up, go to bed, work, and eat meals.

A servant is not one who can take time to develop a personal estate. A servant is engaged in tasks that might be menial compared to his or her own dreams for life to meet the needs of those in charge. If a servant does not accept this discipline willingly, even joyfully, life becomes unbearable. The joy of servanthood only comes through choosing willing submission.

With Jesus, servanthood was a visible denial of privilege or position. His life showed that a servant lives for the other willingly, gladly, joyfully, possibly with suffering. He chose servanthood as his response to the assignment of the cross. But without choice servanthood is slavery. To choose servanthood means one is fully aware of one's own worth and personal powers but willingly yields these up for the sake of the other. Then denial of self becomes redemptive and is not merely a pulling back.

Can an older adult, frail in body and spirit, choose anything? There comes a time when older adults must choose simply to be, to let go and trust without concern about doing. No one need earn his or her way into the family of God. Such relinquishment is also growth.

I believe any job description for a servant of any age should have this freeing corollary: the powerlessness of servanthood does not cause the person to lose a sense of worth and individuality. Regardless of age, every believer is an equal in the kingdom of God.

In a true community of servants, there are no hierarchies of ministries, no dualities, no dichotomies, no difference between served and server, as we have established it today. The ministry is a mutual one in which each person sets the other person free to serve, probably in new and different ways, as long as God grants life and strength. No one group is active and the other passive, one labeled a problem and the other the one with the answers, one tagged the "others" or "they" and rest referred to as "we" and "us."

I can't recall when my friendship with Esther Ebel, an older woman, started. When she was younger, she raised a family, became much involved in church work, and spent years as dean of women of a church-related college. She had been on church building committees and spoke of personally finishing the attic of their home.

In her final years, Esther had one lengthy illness after another. Each brief recovery made it more difficult to find joy to return to life, especially when she found herself tethered to an oxygen tank, her voice weakening and eyesight dimming. "Give me something to think about, Katie," was her most frequent request. "Talk about what you're doing." Sometimes I found her playing Boggle with herself to keep her mind occupied with "good thoughts." Now I had to initiate our prayer-time with which we often ended our visits.

I remember her best for her concern for all generations. She honored her predecessors by her actions and her memory of them. The spring before she died, she and I drove to several cemeteries, where her closest relatives were buried, to retrieve the wreaths she had laid there for Memorial Day. She intended to wash and store them for use next year. She was the faithful keeper of the memories of the departed in her family.

She blessed me and my generation. She had concern for people of her generation. In late life she maintained an active visitation ministry to residents of the Salem Hospital and Home where she resided. When she had strength, she wrote letters to her many friends and "adopted" grandchildren. She sewed small items for gifts, for a relief agency, for the mission circle, and to meet individual needs. I often met a grandson in her home. She served each generation. She clearly demonstrated the servant role of the older adult in completing the life cycle.

An attitude like Esther Ebel's may look like sacrifice. But for the individual, it is the only way or life becomes miserable; one's power is no longer the power of Christ, but only efficient human effort.

What does God have in mind for the older adult? Older adults' vision that Christ can work in the lives of the next generation binds the generations together and completes the life cycle. Their task is to hand the faith on. Now the responsibility belongs to someone else. That enables the older adult to leave in peace.

9

The little old lady in tennis shoes

The older woman, a majority within the older majority, will find herself the determining factor in affecting the quality of life for the entire society.—Elizabeth Welch

The land of aging belongs to little old ladies in tennis shoes, athletic shoes, dress shoes, and slippers. It has become theirs by default. There are more of them. Older women outnumber older men nearly two to one. The sex ratio increases with age, ranging from 123 women to every 100 men for the sixty-five to sixty-nine group to a high of 258 women for every 100 men for persons eighty-five and older. Whether living alone, in nursing homes, or retirement centers, women dominate the land of the elderly by their presence. (Statistics in this chapter are from AARP's "A Profile of Older Americans" based on U.S. Bureau of Census statistics.)

The land of aging belongs to women because older women function better than older men. Betty Friedan in *The Fountain of Age* points out that when a husband dies, older widows adjust to the loss and move on to new strengths with less apparent difficulty than younger women—and less difficulty than men at any age. They get along better psychologically in old age than men do, probably because they've been through other border crossings. They've left behind the strain of cyclic life and having babies. And they've moved on to new things.

A man pulls the plug on his career and the danger of collapsing is great, especially if he has concentrated on success. Many women, especially those who never worked outside the home or worked only part-time, keep on doing what they have always been doing. The pursuit of power has not often been an older woman's goal. And until now retirement has been a male transition.

Women's better mental health in old age can also be attributed to their having had more friends and support groups throughout life. And they maintain them. In our congregation, quilting has long been a tradition. The glue of friendship becomes strong among women who sit around a frame, hour upon hour, week after week, year after year. They're used to sharing their thoughts and feelings.

Though age and growth seem like contradictory terms to some, growth is not a new concept to older women. For the last half century or more, women in our society have focused on growth and generativity. Sewing circles, mission groups, study groups, Bible study fellowships, and special interest groups have been important in their lives. Before women's organizations first started, the women were often socially isolated, especially if they were farm women. This regular gathering with other women kept their lifeblood flowing.

Critics of women's growth movements blame women's steady thirst for knowledge and opportunities to use their skills and gifts as the cause of marriage breakups. For a number of years, women have overshot their husbands in personal development.

Most men like football and basketball. Women like books and getting together with other women. Bookstores attest that women are the biggest readers. And reading is a catalyst for change. Yet some men want women to remain as they were when they married them—unassertive; accepting the husband's role as main family provider, sole leader, and decision-maker. But women refuse to stay put. They have programmed growth into their lives for decades, sometimes by design, sometimes unconsciously.

The land of aging belongs to women because older women, rather than older men, are the core of the volunteer movement, a movement with more older people than young ones. Without women many an organization would collapse. Since moving to Wichita, I have found that any organization that functions with a great deal of volunteer help uses primarily women. Forming auxiliaries is not a male activity. And sociologists point out that women with good self-esteem are the ones who volunteer.

Women enter this stage in life with a new kind of freedom. They have tasted and enjoy the new freedom to discuss their biological functions and sexuality. This year I attended a one-woman musical, *I Am Annie Mae*, in which an African-American woman tells the story of her life in words and song. Born about the turn of the century, she experienced both violent and subtle discrimination from the Jim Crow laws and the Ku Klux Klan. Her life was work, work, work. But the performance also highlighted the joys and pains of simply being human.

One particularly humorous song titled "Rags" salutes the dozens of rags she and her sisters used while menstruating. Her mother washed the rags and carefully hid them under other clothes on the clothesline so that no one would see them.

The audience (mostly women) laughed hilariously. Those of us who were older knew what she was exalting. Our own mothers made homemade pads with cotton-batting lining. Then later they pulled the soiled pads apart to soak, boil, and wash. Still later we saw them fluttering on the line to bleach in the sun. A mother's weekly chore was to turn these rags into another stack of pads. I never heard my mother complain about this task.

I wrote my ninety-eight-year-old mother about the song. When I next phoned her, to my amazement, she chuckled to think about the hundreds of rags that had passed through her hands. And I thought of the love and humility of our mothers who embraced this lowly task for us growing girls. But to uplift this lowly task into a song? No one would have dared when I was young.

This freedom to talk about menstruation is picked up in the musical *Quilters,* in which four young adolescent girls reveal their fears and resentment (an inherited resentment) at beginning the monthly curse of all women, but also their thrill and joy of knowing they were entering womanhood. Speaking openly about menstruation, childbirth, and menopause is a welcome change from regarding a woman's bodily functions as unclean and shameful, to be concealed as if they didn't exist. Young girls today are introduced to these physical changes as a wonderful preparation for motherhood.

Menopause has also come out from under the covers, and with it more openness about rape, domestic abuse, and sexual harassment. When she was in her nineties, Mother told me the story of nearly being raped as a young woman in south Russia, a story she never had the courage to tell me until rape became everyday news.

A group of men of dubious reputation knew she would be walking alone to her home after visiting her grandmother. They hung around. She hid behind the door in the passageway of her grandmother's home and tricked the men into thinking she was gone. Her grandmother then placed her in the custody of a male family friend, who promised to take her home safely. Those were times when young men hid their girlfriends in fields if they knew bands of anarchists were passing through the area.

When I was a young, some women in our immigrant village accepted abuse from their husbands as their lot. If a wife disobeyed, she had to be beaten into place —and the Bible admonished a wife to submit, so she thought. Wife beating is still culturally acceptable in some groups. But this group of women now moving into middle age does not accept abuse as passively as the previous generation did; they do not believe a theology that places submission to husband above personal physical safety.

I think older women do better at aging because they have experienced various lifestyles. They've been single, married, sometimes divorced or widowed. They've been at home; they've worked outside the home. They've worked part-time, they've worked full-time. They may have tried a 1960s lifestyle and given it up for a modified 1990s one.

I can see change coming as I watch my daughters and daughter-in-law manage their lives and those of their families. The media image of older women at one time tended to be "powerless, befuddled, inflexible, and feeble. They also were sexless, since scriptwriters paired older male characters with younger females," writes Sally Steenland in *Media and Values.* But that is changing.

Older female television characters are wealthy, sexy, and face no age discrimination as they grow older. It used to be that women depreciated with age more than men. Men developed a beautiful patina like the family silver, making them more distinguished and attractive. Women just got scratched, dented, and baggy. But no more. Today's older women have better figures than their mothers had. They know more clearly what they want out of life and aren't afraid to go for it.

With the prevalence of divorce, the next generation of older women will head complex families shaped by breakups—divorced parents, divorced children, divorced grandparents. As single parents they have had to make their own decisions and will continue to do so into old age. Elizabeth Welch, in *Learning to Be 85*, states that the number of older women and their varied abilities, as well as their knowledge, skills, and values as both homemakers and career women "combine to furnish the coming century with a diverse source of immeasurable and invaluable strength."

Welch foresees the development of a new matriarchy in baby boomer women. These are women experienced in a variety of skills and in caregiving. One-third of boomer women in their late sixties will have living parents and will function as the center of the family relationship.

These women have known financial independence and enjoy an excellent work record as managers and executives. They have juggled career, children, family, and marriage for several decades. So they will have greater financial security, having built up their own social security deposits. However, whatever problems men with careers face at retirement will also be faced by these women.

Being better at aging than men does not deny the problems older women face. Older women are more likely to be poor than older men. In 1990 women aged sixty-five and older made up 74 percent of the 3.7 million elderly poor. They have always worked at lower average wages than men, many have never worked outside the home, and some have had their work record interrupted by family responsibilities to care for children or sometimes for parents. The average woman spends eighteen years caring for elderly family members and seventeen years caring for children, not at the same time. So the later life income is small for millions of women.

The Social Security system was established in 1935, when the typical family consisted of husband working and wife at home, and so women who began with this system are not always financially secure. The median income of older persons in 1992 was $14,548 for males and $8,189 for females. Nearly three out of four older people living in poverty today are women.

Older women living alone and older unmarried women have especially high poverty rates. Older women had a higher poverty rate (16%) than older men (9%) in 1992. The Census Bureau says one out of five women seventy-five and over was poor in 1992, but only one in ten men was. Elderly poverty was highest among black women seventy-five and over—43 percent of them were poor, compared to 32 percent of Latino women and 18 percent of white women. Older male householders were more likely to be owners of their homes (85%) than were females (68%). More older women than men were employed (61%, 48%).

If poverty is more prevalent among older women than among men, so is aloneness and the sometimes accompanying loneliness. Though they were brought up to believe marriage was the goal, many older women end up living alone. Socially they don't have the same prerogatives as older men to date and marry younger persons. About 42 percent of older women and 16 percent of older men lived alone in 1992. In 1992, older men were nearly twice as likely to be married as older women. Half of older women in 1992 were widows (48%). There were nearly five times as many widows (8.6 million) as widowers (1.9 million).

No, all is not sweetness and light for today's older women. They are physically more vulnerable to crime and fraud. To test a theory about older women, the CBS program *Prime Time* sent a young woman to a jeweler to have some jewelry repaired. The work was satisfactorily done. Then they sent an older woman to the same jeweler for repair work. She was defrauded and a synthetic diamond substituted for her marked real one.

A local editorial writer tells of waiting behind an elderly woman at the local farm produce stand one hot summer day. Everyone around her was waited on. Until someone made room for her, she was not waited on. The produce-stand owners preferred young females. The older women were taken for granted.

I've seen this happen in other settings. Older women waiting for someone to help them hang a heavy picture or move a piece of furniture. Older women waiting in church corners for someone to talk to them. Older women waiting quietly for someone to pick them up and return them to their apartments after church. Older women waiting for a small opportunity to offer their thinking—but they're out of practice, so they remain silent.

Many times I have seen a woman discover enormous inner strengths after the death of her husband or after a divorce. This is especially true for women in the generation who typically did not grow up taking charge of their lives and had not previously developed their own decisiveness, creativity, independence, and courage. Mother accepted Dad's death with sorrow and equanimity. She was glad he died first, for she knew she would cope better than he.

Betty Friedan, in *The Fountain of Age*, attributes the better mental health of today's older women to the women's movement toward equality. In the last decades, women have received the freedom to choose career with or without marriage. With choice comes self-responsibility and empowerment, something closed to an earlier generation of women. Friedan states that something wonderful happens when women finally get to the point of affirming themselves, or, as poet Maya Angelou says it, of thinking "nobly" of themselves.

But this is no new truth. Jesus spoke of loving our neighbor "as ourselves." When older women love themselves, no one will be able to rob them of their right to spiritual growth and the use of spiritual gifts.

Until her death in March 1994, my favorite older woman for many years was my mother. What did I learn from my mother? What do I hope my children, especially my daughters, learned from me and are learning from me as an older woman?

As a child, I thought my mother was old when she was in her forties because she was already plump. Young people were skinny, old people were fat to have better laps for children to sit on. I considered Mother old when I was a child because she wore a corselette with stays and lacing (not just a girdle) for which she went to a Spirella Company agent to be fitted. All her life, she swore that it gave her body strength (and shaped her figure).

My mother, a widow for about seven years, told me of her years of loneliness as a new immigrant to this country. With five small children and no English language skills, she was isolated from adults, except for my father, who spent most of each day at his store. She began learning to speak and read English with us children.

She also told me how she ventured out in the community, into women's church organizations and the Red Cross. And found she had gifts to contribute in her baking, knitting, and sewing abilities, and in her love of ideas. So she developed these gifts and was affirmed for them.

Cooking was her ministry of choice. A well-prepared meal was her gift of love, warmth, and intimacy. She always spoke of making "my dinner." That meal belonged to her until she gave it away. Meals were always eaten at the table where everyone had a place. "Eat, eat," she admonished us children.

When we grew older, we rebelled at her pushing food at us. But I sense now this was her way to give us herself. She taught me how to manage a home. I did not learn to cook and bake at home, for that was her domain. But I learned that a home only functions well when someone is in control of its management. She was.

She taught me how to sacrifice for others without considering it a hardship. She made many concessions, too many, I thought, when she longed to speak out. At times I have tried to separate myself from such a self-sacrificing role, but I also draw close to it. For only through sacrifice is the natural turned into the spiritual. She gave us children her untiring devotion and her few possessions.

She gave away nearly everything she owned to keep things from cluttering her home and becoming a burden to whoever had to clean up her estate. Through the years she gave what she didn't need to whomever it was most convenient to give it to—children, grandchildren, or even the man who came to mow the lawn. She wanted to leave this earth with as few of this world's goods left behind as possible. "There's still so much to clean up," she mentioned to me a few weeks before her death.

She believed in prayer. She often talked about wrestling with Satan about discouragement. For a woman with limited education, she enjoyed a rich intellectual and spiritual life. She read many books and church newspapers, which always lay scattered around her. She called them her "friends."

I remember Mother's acceptance of the burden of being biblically submissive to my father, a submission so uncompromising she denied herself close friendships with other women, especially after his retirement. He needed her. He didn't like to go visiting. So she didn't go either.

She was a husband-oriented woman who saw her God-given calling to be caretaker of her life partner and children. She laid out Dad's underwear and clothing before he had his bath, just like she helped us choose what we were to wear when we were children. She offered him a clean handkerchief in the morning, advised him when his store apron needed to be replaced, and told him when to go to the barber. He learned to depend on her for personal care.

She never criticized him nor allowed us to criticize him, for she knew how hard he worked and how much we as a family depended on his wage-earning skills to survive. She protected him from us when we complained. She protected him from society, excusing him on the grounds of his many obligations when he felt judged for never having become wealthy. She lived through him and us. She had never expected to do anything else in life.

Father's task was to keep a roof over our heads, clothing on our bodies, and food on the table. Hers was to keep the family together. The emotional well-being, spiritual guidance, protection from disease and moral danger, and happiness or unhappiness of the family rested on her shoulders.

She gave herself little room to develop outside the parameters she had established for her role in life. Later she found it impossible to change her habits, even after Dad died. She had wrapped her life up in his, and now she had no courage to risk new friends. She had assured him daily by her actions she loved him. She had prayed he would die before her. When he was gone, her main role in life was finished.

Like many other people of her time, Mother governed her life by what image other people would carry in their minds of her and her family. Would they approve? Disapprove? Maintaining an honorable reputation in a small village where a few unfortunates sometimes became the butt of ridicule was a prime virtue. A blight of some kind on the family name and reputation was her greatest fear.

A former acquaintance once mentioned that she and her sister, both elderly and living together, never put the light on at night even for an emergency. They feared the neighbors might think something was wrong. They used flashlights or other lighting in an emergency.

I thought of Mother. She lived in a highrise senior citizens apartment building. She told me that even though she awakened early in the morning, she never got up until about seven for fear of disturbing her neighbors. She lay quietly in her bed until a respectable hour so no one could say she disturbed their sleep. The specter of gossip controlled her thought and actions.

Margaret R. Miles writes in a *Christian Century* essay that our mothers were "the primary source of our socialization to attitudes and behavior," attitudes and behavior we daughters may now resist.

> Although the task of sorting the gifts and handicaps inherited from them may be difficult and lifelong, there is loss in failing to engage the task. Our mothers are within us, close to the bone, for better and for worse. To understand them is to understand something crucial in ourselves. To exorcise some of their constraints while exercising their strengths is to appropriate our own power.

My mother is within me, close to my bone, for better or for worse. I may never fully understand my mother and the constraints which determined her life. I know I have worked to exercise the strengths she has passed on to me, even while I exorcise the constraints, especially worrying what the people will think of me if I depart from traditional ways. I want to claw that attitude, which is bone of my bone, out of my innermost and bury it with her.

Yet I thank her for showing me how to live with change. When I used to phone her, I asked what she had been thinking about during the day. She spent hours, I think, reviewing her life—what it was, what it became, and where she was now going. She mentioned often that she was not afraid to die. And she marveled at the changes she had known. From horse and buggy travel to airplane. From cooking in a wall oven with straw to an electric range. From hand-carried letters to telephone and more.

Little old women like her are without price. Their number is legion. Like the virtuous woman of Proverbs 31, she and other older women are to be praised.

10

Back to my roots

The present contains nothing more than the past, and what is found in the effect was already in the cause. —Henri Bergson

I knew that older people are expected to think nostalgically about the past and wasn't surprised when I found myself thinking about my own background. Where had my ancestors come from? What were they like? How had they influenced who I am today?

I gave myself a retirement gift—a trip to the former Soviet Union, to the land Mother and Dad used to call home. My own border crossing needed a crossing of geographic borders to this land I had heard much about during my childhood.

Call it a return to my roots, if you will—the homing instinct returning. This trip would be no usual tourist travel, with overnight stays in luxury hotels and lounging by the seashore. It would be a journey to the land of people struggling for freedom. A large number of our tour group hoped to visit the specific places where their parents and grandparents had lived in the Ukraine, even though these areas were usually closed to tourist travel.

I wanted to locate relatives who had been forcibly re-turned from Germany to the Soviet Union after World War II. The Yalta agreement decreed that Berlin be divided into four zones and that all Russian-born citizens return to the land of their birth, whether they wanted to or not. What kind of people had I come from on my mother's side? What were my roots?

My knowledge of my mother's branch of the family was limited. Only she and one brother out of twelve chil-dren had come to Canada after World War I. Many family members, particularly the men, had died in the army or concentration camps. Five aunts had managed to survive. Three aunts were still alive, two in the Soviet Union, one in Germany. I was hoping to see one or two face-to-face. Maybe even a cousin or more.

When we travel to an overseas country, we usually ex-pect to return with a suitcase full of souvenirs and other treasures. I bought a few souvenirs, like a woolen shawl and some nesting dolls, but the gifts I received that could not have been bought with money are more valuable to me as I try to retrieve my past. Their only value is in shar-ing them with others.

In the distant city of Novisibirsk, about seven time zones from Moscow, a young married couple gave me a nickel-plated Russian *samovar*, or tea urn. When I returned through United States customs, the agent at the X-ray ma-chine sent the box through twice, trying to figure out what I was bringing back. He finally decided to let it pass.

My parents hand-carried a samovar similar to this one all the way from the Ukraine to Saskatchewan, Canada, in 1923. Their trip began with a converted boxcar cleaned and arranged to allow for sleeping quarters. The immigrants cooked tea but also potatoes and eggs in this tea urn. Then followed an ocean voyage across the Atlantic and another train trip across Canada. My uncles, then pre-teenage boys, carried the bulky samovar in the tin cradle in which my six-month-old sister slept at night.

The samovar with the many strange medallions decorating the front always stood in the corner of our home on a small table, almost like a little shrine. It stood in my mother's living room until she died, although it is no longer used. But it has been and continues to be the single strongest reminder of where our family originated.

It was a good past. A happy past. That is, until the revolution of 1917-1919 shattered everything.

My parents grew up in the Mennonite village of Rosenthal, adjoining the city of Chortitza in the Ukraine, in a thriving economy and culture. The community enjoyed prosperous industry—flour mills, farm machinery factories, brick factories, and more. Wealthy landowners had built magnificent homes and farms near the village. Many schools and institutions and large, well-built, well-attended churches graced the countryside. One artist has depicted this period of gracious living with a volume of photographs titled *Forever Summer, Forever Sunday*.

I met my Aunt Neta in Moscow in a small apartment, where she lives with her daughter and family. She described a Sunday morning in the village as one of her most pleasant childhood memories. In the calm morning, the people, dressed in Sunday clothes, sauntered to church down the clean, tree-lined streets. Birds warbled their good-morning to the worshipers. The sun beamed down. Before long, the voices of the congregation, lifted in praise to God, filled the morning air. As she spoke, I sensed that in her imagination she was transported to her childhood.

My mother and father lived near a small windmill at the edge of Rosenthal, for my father was a miller for part of his life. The windmill stood high on a hill overlooking the village. Ten bags of grain were ground into eleven bags of flour or meal. The miller received the eleventh bag as payment. We children heard many stories about that windmill during our childhood, for it was the center of the Funk family's life.

In a letter to my father before he died, I asked why the windmill stood at the highest place. "To have free wind," he answered, "not sheltered by houses." Wind needs freedom to blow with power. I carried that gift of a samovar home as a reminder of those better times of freedom in the lives of these people and the kind of life they then thought would never leave them. And it symbolized for me how easily the freedom, the peacefulness, the affluence we enjoy may be taken and exchanged for heartache and suffering.

Shoes are important to us. I look down at my feet. I would hardly think of going anywhere without shoes. I've seen college women move into the dormitories with several dozen boxes of shoes. Restaurants display signs, "No shoes, no shirt, no service."

In literature, shoes often become a symbol of belonging. The African-American spiritual states, "When we get to heaven, we gonna put on our shoes; we're gonna walk all over God's heaven." Here in America, as slaves the blacks often went barefoot. Anyone less than a full human being didn't need shoes.

My father knew the meaning of shoes as a symbol of belonging. He grew up wearing *Schlorre*, a kind of wooden sole with a leather band over the toes. As soon as he was old enough, he was expected to make his own, usually from willow wood. Young children inherited an older sibling's *Schlorre*.

Rich people wore shoes; poor people wore these wooden-soled sandals or went barefoot. As a young boy, my father yearned for a pair of shoes. One long summer he tended a close relative's cattle and dreamed about buying shoes with his earnings. But at the end of the summer he received only one ruble. Bitterly disappointed, he ran home mourning the loss of his dream.

As a medic in the Russian Red Cross during World War I, Father was issued real leather boots. He buried these boots after the Russian revolution so no anarchist would steal them from him. Footwear was in desperately short supply. Everyone wanted boots. One day a revolutionary forced him at gunpoint to dig up whatever he had hidden, and that was the end of his wonderful boots.

In Moscow I spent long hours talking to my mother's sister, Aunt Neta. She and my mother hadn't seen each other in sixty-seven years and never did. Aunt Neta also grew up in the Ukraine. But after World War II, in the fall of 1943, she had made it as far as Berlin together with four sisters and their children. It was a long and difficult trek, first following the German army back to Poland, then on to Germany.

Some German-speaking settlers from Russia escaped into the American Zone of Berlin. But my five aunts (all widows) and their families were deported in unheated cattle cars with hundreds of other Germans to the never-ending forests of central Asia at the end of the war.

I had never fully understood the term "Siberia." Geographers think of it as 6 million square miles of steppes, forest, and tundra, beginning approximately at the Ural Mountains, stretching thousands of miles to the Pacific and north to the Arctic Sea. Other people think of it as I did—a less defined but fearful wilderness to which the Soviet regime exiled dissidents as punishment and to develop its mineral and forest resources.

In the forests of Siberia, these exiled German-speaking people, derided as Nazi lovers, were forced to work outdoors on ground that was soft peat in summer and deep snow in winter. They lacked adequate footwear. My cousin told me of standing barefoot in fresh cowpies in cool weather for a few seconds of warmth. People's feet froze in the bitterly cold weather. What to do?

A kind Russian woman observed these people from the Ukraine without adequate shoes and introduced them to *Lappchen*—a kind of fitted snowshoe woven out of bark. The feet were first wrapped with cloths and then these *Lappchen* were bound on the foot around the cloths. Lifesavers. They could walk on the peat and the snow. My aunt said she had traded two pairs of men's underwear for one pair of *Lappchen*.

I met many other people who had been deported to this area during those Stalinist years. Late one evening, at the request of a nephew, three of us visited ninety-one-year-old David Klassen. He had possibly known my mother as a young man. Both had worked in the same mental health institution during the revolution.

At the entrance to the high-rise apartment building, children played in the courtyard. Old women wearing babushkas sat on a bench and watched us. The daughter of David Klassen and her family were planning to migrate to Germany, so many household belongings were packed. Rugs had been rolled up and boxes stood half-full.

His family woke the old man up and put a shirt on him so he could sit up in bed. He was blind and almost totally deaf. With hearing aids unavailable to him, we shouted through a rolled-up newspaper to try to get him to hear us. Once it became clear to him why we were there and that I wanted to hear something about his early life, his mind became as clear as yesterday. This preacher, musician, and poet had been exiled three times (eleven, five, and two-and-a-half years) for preaching. His wife had spent ten years in exile for attending church. When she was taken, the children had clung to the wagon, but the soldiers had whipped their hands.

As we rose to leave, he took my hands in his, wept and kissed them, grateful that someone from America would visit him. His nephew requested prayer before we left. The old man insisted on standing "to the glory of God" for prayer. To sit while praying was dishonoring to God. I saw him as a true man of faith, like the elderly Simeon in the temple, waiting to be united with Christ in glory.

Three members of our group went to the home of his nephew, Johann Koop, and his wife and their son and his wife. I found them open and friendly. He was the leader of the then largest Russian Baptist church in the area. Membership had fallen from 1,400 to 1,000 because of the mass migrations to Germany of people who had originally had German ancestors. And it would continue to fall.

He had been deported to this area as a young man of seventeen to work in the mines. Women, sometimes well into a pregnancy, also worked in the mines and forests in the early years. When his group first arrived, they met secretly with Russian Christians. Gradually the group grew. As they had more religious freedom, they built a church.

While I was in that area, I heard story after story of suffering—physical, psychological, and spiritual—but the miracle is that the church of Jesus Christ survived and is now growing.

"We suffered," Koop said. "It was in God's will. I have no hatred, no bitterness about the past. The important thing is to be obedient. They are responsible for what they did. I am responsible for how I responded."

I found people who had learned to believe in God, not for what they could get out of God, but because God is sovereign. They trusted in God even when personal circumstances were against them. They would not be defeated by the forces of evil.

When my aunt tried to explain the woven footwear to me, I couldn't grasp what she was explaining. When I came again the next day, she gave me a pair to take home. I cherish them as a symbol of the suffering of the people of the Soviet Union and the victory of the church of Jesus Christ in the face of that suffering.

A third item I couldn't pack in a suitcase. I didn't need to. I returned with countless stories people told me about their lives. I came back with a renewed sense of the importance of story, especially for the older adult. Stories bind the generations together. Stories bring light to dense abstractions. Stories show the pattern of living. Stories assert boldly, "I am a human being."

I think back to the time we as a church used to have story-times. We called it testimony time. I recall the same people, usually people with reputation for piety, getting up every time—either out of loyalty to the leader or out of loyalty to themselves. Someone had to show some spiritual vitality. The others stayed silent.

Many people had few new spiritual experiences to talk about. The stories became stereotyped, dead, and lifeless testimonies. The leader asked for popcorn testimonies and if you didn't have anything to say, shout out a Bible verse, anything. Say something. I sometimes wracked my brain to say something spiritually bright and witty. Instead of stories, we heard mechanical words trying to shape peppy, happy little testimonies about hoped-for faith or about life as the speakers expected or wanted it to be. There was little weeping of God's tears of sorrow and repentance.

Slowly the story and the beliefs drifted apart. We defended fiercely what we believed, down to the fine points, even if we didn't always know why.

The linear story of God's dealings with humanity from Genesis to Revelation—what God has done, is doing, and will continue to do—has never became one unified account for some people. The grandeur of the story of how God comes to human beings in the history of God's people escapes them.

Their strong meat is some aspect of the systems that have grown out the stories: Does a human being have a two- or three-part nature? Did Judas have free choice if he had to be the traitor?

The Israelites were a story-built people. A study of the Old Testament soon reveals that their faith was built upon stories of their experiences with God. The events they looked back to included the exodus, the wanderings in the wilderness, the conquest of Canaan, and the experiences of their leaders like David and Solomon and many others. We have the idea that faith is built on propositional truth, yet these theological principles actually developed out of stories. Stories came first.

The truer statement about our faith is always our personal story—and that is what I found in the Soviet Union. Here story and faith came together. What the people experienced about God showed up in their personal history. And that holds true for me. What I have experienced with God shows up in my history. If I believe in forgiveness, my history will have stories of reconciliation with husband, children, friends, and neighbors.

In the Soviet Union, wherever I went—if someone had two minutes to spare while waiting for a meal or a service to start, sitting on a bus, driving to an appointment—someone was telling me their story. A retired school teacher who lives on a small pension escorted me to my hotel one afternoon to meet relatives while the other tour members went on to visit a university. We walked along the riverbank, sat on the park benches (he spread a handkerchief for me to sit on), and talked. He recited poems, his own and those he had translated into Russian from German.

He had kept many notes of his life in exile. As we discussed Solzhenitsyn's *One Day in the Life of Ivan Denisovich*, he commented, "I have experienced all of that." He had a secret manuscript of his experiences in a work camp. When I left, he wanted to give me something to remind me of him and his story. He offered me his comb, the only thing he carried he could part with, and he needed even that item, for he was poor. His story may never get published, but it is a compelling affirmation of his existence as a human being when those in power treated him as less than an animal. It is a cry for justice.

If we as a community of faith lose our stories, along with them we lose the power and the glory of the good news, for in the story lies the essence of our faith. Stories distilled and organized and packaged for popular consumption in the form of theological systems do not capture the imagination for the listener.

If you ask me to tell you about my God, I might answer with my confession of faith—God is loving, forgiving, redeeming. When I tell you my story, I tell you about the God I actually worship. True faith is revealed in our story.

The faith that I heard about in the former Soviet Union was no magic-genie-in-a-lamp kind of faith, but a deeply rooted understanding that though all hell had broken loose around them, God was still on his throne. And they would continue to worship the sovereign God of history.

When someone tells their story, the storyteller gives the listeners a gift. My aunt, now in her eighties, spent most of two days that I could spend with her giving me the gift of her life. Though her life has been incredibly hard because of two wars, a revolution, and a government that tossed its citizens about like confetti and swept them into the trash bins as easily, she continues to believe.

I felt humbled to know I belonged to her and her family. She is a person who reads widely, is interested in people and ideas, and has staunch convictions. She refused to have anything to do with the government-registered church. "Have we gone through all this suffering for nothing?" she asked. Her nonbelieving son-in-law admitted she lived what she believed.

In Santa Fe, New Mexico, the souvenir shops sell statues of an older man with dozens of little children perched all over his body. The name of this man is "The Storyteller." A society that treasures storytellers is a rich society, a family that encourages storytelling is a rich family. An elder's story, my story, your story, is never completed until life ends, and until then it must be told to pass the riches on to the next generation.

I returned to Kansas more fully aware that, even as I have told other life stories, now telling the story of my transition, my border crossing, was an important task at this stage. The sorting of life experiences is part of the crossing, no, *is* the crossing. And it is my gift to others. I was ready to keep telling.

11

Place: The anchor of memory

Once in his life a man [or woman] ought to con-
centrate his mind upon the remembered earth.
He ought to give himself up to a particular land-
scape in his experience. —Belden C. Lane

Our tour bus pulled up alongside the highway and stopped. I was already waiting beside the driver, directing him where to stop. I stepped out hastily with my camera ready and ran ahead to the highest point I could go without crawling over and under fences. This stop was just for me; the rest of the tour group waited in the bus.

The evening before I left for the former Soviet Union, I had phoned my mother in Edmonton, Alberta. Once again she had given me instructions how to find the spot where the Funk windmill once stood at the edge of the village of Rosenthal. "Follow the main road from Chortitza through Rosenthal to the top of the hill. That's where your father and I once lived."

Now here I was, at the top of the hill, taking in a view I had never expected to see. This was the same panorama my parents saw when they had stood on this spot about seventy years ago as a young married couple. Behind me lay the city of Rosenthal and the adjoining city of Chortitza.

Somewhere close to where I now stood had once been the Funk family windmill—a black and white pen drawing of which had hung in my parents' home for decades and an etched copy of which now hung in my living room.

My grandfather had owned this windmill, built high on the steppes to catch the prevailing winds. My father and his brothers had worked in it while growing up and had become familiar with windmills, winds, and people who came to have their grain ground.

Decades ago, from the top of this high hill, you could see the farmsteads, the steam flour mill, brick factories, shops, schools, and the hospital in Chortitza. The Funk home was the last one at which the village cowherd blew his horn each morning, calling them to let out their cow so it could join the others he was taking to the common pasture beyond the village limits. Now I saw the tall buildings of a more modern city and rolling hills.

Dad talked about this windmill a great deal as we children grew up. It became a symbol to us children of another home, another time, another way of living, far away. My brother named a small family newspaper *The Funk Windmill*. This place high on a windy hill had shaped Dad's identity, his view of life, and his thinking about how God worked in people's lives. From the time he was a boy, he went daily from this place high on the hill to school, to church, to town, to work, to the army during the war, to a period of voluntary service after the war. He brought his bride, my mother, here. Together they left this place to make a home in a new land—Canada.

After he and Mother were married, they lived in the

corner-room (*Eckstoav*) in Dad's parental home for most of their first two years together. My sisters Frieda and Anne were conceived in that corner room in the ropebed. Frieda was born there. In that house he prepared the sermon he would later preach often, comparing the ways of the wind to the working of the Holy Spirit in a person's life. "The wind blows wherever it pleases. You hear its sound, but you cannot tell where it comes from or where it is going. So it is with everyone born of the Spirit." He believed that. He had no patience with people who held that the Holy Spirit could be confined to a circumscribed path. He knew the ways of the wind from the time he was a child.

All Dad's stories about Rosenthal flooded my mind as I surveyed the scene at the top of the hill. I wanted to say to the bus driver, "Go on and leave me here. I want to imprint every hill, tree, and valley in my mind." But the tour group waited patiently as I tried to fill the reservoirs of my memory with what I was seeing and connect it to what I had heard from my father.

The whole trip to Russia was a return to my roots. Why are middle-aged and older adults obsessed with the past, and particularly with the places of their origin? Russia does not have holy shrines like in Jerusalem to which people make pilgrimages. So why this travel by American descendants of people who once lived in that country to their birthplaces? Or in North America, why do older adults search for years for the place they once lived?

With me on tour were other older adults, hunting their roots, the places where their ancestors had once established homes, made history, and been buried. It becomes clearer to me as I grow older that memory and meaning is linked to place and that both are important as one grows older. This was another step in my border crossing.

I've gone back to my own childhood home in Canada. About a decade ago I returned to the small village of Blaine Lake in northern Saskatchewan, to drive up and down its streets. I returned especially to take another look at the once proudly-owned cream, brown, and green house where I grew up but which would soon be bulldozed and replaced with a modern home. I and my siblings can talk at length about this place. It has taken on the mystical qualities of Peter Pan's Never-Never Land, even though we know our house was small, overcrowded, without evidence of wealth, and the scene of many battles and heartaches.

When I return to Hillsboro, I frequently drive past the three houses where we once lived—the one where my husband died, the one where I and my children brought one another up, the one where I lived after the children left home.

The children seldom refer to the first house where we lived two years and where my husband died. My daughter Christine went back to 308 West Grand on a recent vacation. It's still a big, drafty, two-story frame rental house overrun by untrimmed trees and shrubs. A little girl was playing outside. As Christine talked to her briefly, a glass dropped from the porch and broke. She helped the little girl gather the pieces. To Christine, the little incident was symbolic of her life at 308 West Grand, where death broke our family.

Then she drove to 208 North Jefferson, our second home, but didn't stare too hard at this much-renovated ranch-style house. In this house we began to come to terms with the fact that we were a single-parent family. We worked to turn this place into a home.

The North Jefferson house became a place of memories—good and bad. We had the largest bathroom in Hillsboro, we were sure. A Quonset hut had been remodeled into a house, and one of the bedrooms was turned into a bathroom. We liked this huge bathroom, although visitors often seemed surprised when they stepped into it. It became the gathering place for family visiting as the girls did their hair and hand-laundry or found someone to talk to.

Christine memorialized it in a poem:

To Mother on Moving Day

Mother dear,
before you lock the door the last time
and leave this funeral for our past
pause
listen to:
the bathroom
sobbing with more pathos than any mourner
in the process of rooms.

Hear the shower gush a wet outburst
on patient porcelain, hollowed
by endless pink bottoms,
and the toilet tank sighing to the end
of its rushing and flushing.

Think of the silver faucets dripping their quiet tears
on rusty stoppers, remembering
a million morning splashes.

The mirror knows
we will no longer crowd its liquid surface
with the O's of our eyes and curlers.

How the mirror shudders when you slam the door.

But slam the door for the last time we did. The two-yard lot proved my undoing when it came to mowing the grass. I moved alone to 103 East B. Each child had found a spot elsewhere. The truck brought everything I owned materially to my third Hillsboro home, a duplex, in which I lived more or less by myself.

When I moved to Wichita after nine years, I again moved into a duplex and again chose the north side, causing grandson David, who came to visit from Connecticut, to comment, "It looks just like the old place." Why did I choose the north side? I think that, among other reasons, the main one was that it would mean disruption of fewest patterns of living if I placed all my furniture and looked at the morning sun the same way I had in Hillsboro.

Homesickness, nostalgia for one's childhood birth-place, one's home, and one's home country represents a longing for a place where one felt at home, where one had life-changing experiences, where one knew love and understanding, memories that cannot be forgotten. In Marquez' *One Hundred Years of Solitude* is a village in which the people have the disease of forgetting. They forget anything and everything. So a young man posts a sign at the entrance to the village that gives the name of the village and says, "There is a God." If the villagers forgot either, they would not survive. A home is a place you can always return to, even if only in memory.

It becomes clear to me that to understand fully my aging I have to come to terms with the significance of place in my life. I was moving to Wichita into another separate residence of my own. But many other people at this stage move to a retirement center, some to a nursing home, some to live with children. What makes this traumatic? What makes the move easier?

People who have suffered loss of home through flood, tornado, or hurricane can teach us why moves for older adults are difficult. These people soon discover that regardless of whether they owned or rented the property, damage to personal space has "a spiritual dimension," write Carl S. Dudley and Melvin E. Schoonover in "After the Hurricane" (*Christian Century*, June 2-9, 1993). Healing began for people who lost all in Hurricane Andrew when they "acknowledged their grief for lost space and reconstructed at least symbolic fences to create a place that they could call their own."

Loss of place meant loss of familiar patterns of living, but it also meant loss of irreplaceable heirlooms—items of personal significance such as pictures, diplomas, childhood trophies, memorabilia of an earlier age—all of which are symbols of events that can be recalled but never explained. I have a small stack of these items so valueless monetarily, so hard to discard.

At the heart of the faith-life is the ability to recall experiences with God, which are usually also experiences of places where one got along or didn't get along with other people. We carry within us our own memories of places important to us but also memories of places shared with us by parents, grandparents, and people we have known or read about. I carry my parents' memories of their life on that hill in Russia even as they did. My Russian roots lie deep within me.

In the Old Testament, God clearly connects himself to the Israelites and to a place—Canaan. The land was their inheritance. Theologian Walter Brueggeman writes that in the Old Testament there is no timeless space and also no spaceless time—there is only storied place. Abraham left Ur and risked homelessness to gain a home. In Egypt the

Israelites had a deep yearning for a home, but their actions led to homelessness. They spent four hundred years in Egypt and later another forty years in the place we know as the wilderness because of their lack of faith.

The New Testament does not seem to have as close a link to geographic place. Here faith is spiritual and non-geographical. Children of God are children of God's household. Yet the apostle Peter writes a letter to the geographically scattered Christians, people who belong to some other land and are temporarily residing with a people to whom they do not belong.

I assert again that places are the anchors of memory. Meaningful experience at any age is always "placed" experience. To listen to stories is to sense this at once. Those who wrench their experience from a setting and say only, "The Lord blessed me this week," utter empty words, copycat words.

I believe older people are trying to tell us something about place but don't have the words and courage to say that to be housed in a safe warm place with sufficient food and good medical attention is not enough. If they have a commitment to that new place, they will try to make it enough. The Israelites experienced the "enoughness" of God's presence in the desert.

But it doesn't feel like home. Until one has lived long enough in a place to have built up memories in it, it isn't home. And older people know that when they enter a nursing home at age eighty-five or older, they haven't much time to make it a place of rich memories. It becomes a place of silent waiting to go to the next home in glory.

God is assuredly a God of place, not just of time. A longing for a place of one's own is a human hunger, whether the person is five years old or ninety-five. Little children make a "home" out of empty cardboard boxes, a few boards, a blanket over chairs. But older adults can't do that. To move into a new place when quite old is a move toward dropping out of the history of an identifiable people in an identifiable pilgrimage.

Consequently, many older people in retirement centers feel displaced. The problem is not lack of warmth and security; those needs are met. The problem is that no one is there to receive them and their ideas, their feelings, their very beings.

Once when I was visiting my mother, I went with her to the dining hall of the nursing home next door to her apartment building. Older men and women sat at tables, mostly silent, waiting patiently for their food, unable to break the barriers between them though some had lived in this place a long time. They had few joint experiences to talk about, no joint goals, and no plans to continue traditions. They had little interest in one another.

And we children, who were there with our parents, exclaimed about the excellence of the food and the beauty of the environment and the wonderful weather. They agreed, without emotion. But it wasn't like hosting a family gathering in a home with everyone bringing bowls of food, and grandchildren dashing about and getting under grown-ups' feet and slamming doors. How does one develop family traditions when time is slipping by much too quickly and children and grandchildren visit only occasionally or not at all?

Why was this spot on the top of the hill, in southern Ukraine, now a wheatfield, so important to Dad as he grew older? He talked about it often. The answers become clearer. He had exchanged important words of covenant with God, with self, with others in this place. Family history had been created there. That space had historical significance for him—and much more. Events had happened that he later remembered and that provided continuity for his life.

He spoke important words in those rooms that established his identity for all his life and gave him a vision of his future. He had exchanged vows there and made promises and even demands that formed his character. Something had been expected of him there. As a young man of twenty-five, he had been undertaker, preacher, and chief mourner for four of his close relatives who died during a typhus epidemic. In this place he had promised my mother that some day when the political situation eased he would search for a family he had never met, her missing family lost in the Russian revolution.

Name and place of birth is important to identification at border crossings between countries. It is important in the eyes of the law—identity is tied to it. The assumption always is that you have a fixed address—you are not homeless. Name and place of birth is important to my identification at my border crossing.

Everyone who lived in that modest home behind the mill knew his or her name as something more than a laundry label. Birthplace identifies a culture and biological characteristics. Father was Jasch Funk, the miller's son.

Here on this site where I stood in the Ukraine, there was always a spot for Dad at the table, even during the most difficult times of the revolution and the famine. Whatever food was available would be shared.

Dad's younger brother recalls that the year after their father died of typhus during the height of the famine, they had come down to the breakfast table at Christmas expecting a gift as usual, even though they knew their mother's resources were limited. At each place at the table lay a small item wrapped in a twist of paper. They unwrapped their gifts to find each child had a small cube of dry white bread, which their mother had saved for them for this special day. That morning the boys had licked at their cubes, happy, and they wondered why their mother cried.

In Robert Frost's poem, *The Hired Man*, the farmer says to his wife, "Home is the place where, when you have to go there, they have to take you in." His wife replies, "I should have called it something you somehow haven't to deserve." That matched Dad's definition of a home as he had experienced it at the windmill spot.

But I return to the question facing many older adults. What is the solution to the uncomfortable feeling for some that life is closing in when moving from big place to smaller place to still smaller place? Some people cry with the children of Israel, "How can we sing the songs of Zion in a strange land?" My advice to myself is to stay independent as long as possible, but not so independent I isolate myself from other people's love and refuse to make moves that become necessary because of medical problems.

I assure myself that God cannot be comfortably contained in any one place, big or small, forever and ever. He was with my father in South Russia but also in Canada. He was with us at 308 West Grand, but also at 208 North Jefferson and at 103 East B. A place is holy when it helps to bring to pass God's purposes. God can meet me even if I'm not on my own turf.

God can meet me in times of transition and in geographic places that are caught in transition. Many life decisions are made in situations of displacement or even limitation, such as a camp or conference. No fixed place can fully contain the holy. God walks freely among those who turn to him. God is not limited by human efforts to manage the mystery of God.

Our culture has come to accept that there is a place for each person. From the time we are children we begin this search for our place—a place of security, acceptance, identity, and happiness. Young or old, we keep looking.

As a young girl, I used to lie on the sunny side of the woodpile in the backyard, gazing at the blue skies decorated with free-floating clouds, wondering about the place I would have someday in life. The woodpile is long gone, but the desire for a place remains no matter how old I am.

Each spring as I watch summer gaining strength, I know I will miss my children's attempts at place-making when they were young. How long has it been since they last hauled out blankets, tarps, and clothespins to create a tent over the clothesline? Most of their energy was devoted to frantic pinning and stretching, very little to sitting in the airtight compartment that resulted. Sweaty and tired, they sometimes relaxed briefly to munch crackers and drink Kool-Aid in their "own place."

This longing for an emotional niche where we can be free to be ourselves, to love, and to risk failure is almost instinctive. To lose it means to stop growing and become stagnant. Yet somehow most of us believe that when we find this place where we will fit in, it will turn out to be a ledge, a stopping point on life's journey. It will be an arriving. And often that last comfortable place where we consciously made memories as an older adult becomes that ledge and with it comes the temptation to say firmly, "I am not going to budge again."

What then is the older Christian's place? The Christian's place, young or old, is preparation for the next step, as it was for Abraham and Moses. It is to be on a journey. And on this journey, God will take care of us.

12

Tilling the soil of memory

The destiny of the world is determined less by the battles that are lost and won than by the stories it loves and believes in. —Harold Goddard

In the years before his death, my father was doing an informal life review, which is an important aspect of growing older. My father had told us children countless stories of his growing up to make sense of the atrocities and absurdities of his past as a child of the Russian steppes and a young man living in very disturbed times. He worked hard to deal with his yesteryears—the upheaval caused by the war and revolution, a series of deaths of close relatives, famine, migration, lack of education, and feelings of inferiority.

I thought I knew all of Dad's stories, but obviously there were some so deeply hidden even he didn't have full access to them himself. In a late-life talk with my brother, he had been able to free himself before he died of one more experience in which he had been imprisoned by the Red army and nearly shot.

Several years ago literary critic Alfred Kazin told a conference of English teachers that one writes "to make a home for oneself on paper—to find a place, a ledge." People tell stories to find a place, a ledge, a place of security: "This much I know—this part of my life is secure. I can talk about it. Now how do I deal with the next part that I don't quite understand?"

Kazin spoke particularly about the immigrant child, and he was one. "Language is the salvation of the immigrant child who must reorder his or her existence by means from within." Immigrants have only language by which to pass on what is important to them to the next generation. Their former life in the old country is gone, as frequently also are family heirlooms and artifacts. The territory in the new land is entirely new. All immigrants retain is memories, a value system, and hope for the future.

But most older adults in our country today are not immigrants, although their parents may have been. But we tend to forget that in an era of fast change, we are all immigrants, young and old. The pace of technology has revolutionized our lives. Socially we live in a global village. Older adults have moved often in their lifetime, have probably changed professions and maybe even spouses several times, not to mention values and theological systems. Patterns of life have sometimes been disturbed to the roots by modern change. But they have adapted.

Today, because long life is an unexpected gift to my generation, we are immigrants to the land of the aging. We have as much work to do in life review as my father had to do to come to terms with his difficult past. Telling memories is important to bring about acceptance of the past.

Dag Hammarskjold at age forty-seven, a few months prior to his election as general secretary of the United Nations, wrote in his journal, "Never, 'for the sake of peace

and quiet,' deny your own experience or convictions"
(*Markings*). This entry appears in the midst of several en-
tries about his profound loneliness.

The life review process makes room for experience
and convictions and keeps affirming that life has meaning
even though loneliness reigns and death may be close. Life
review is part of letting go, even as one has to let go of
friends, spouse, health and vigor, lifestyle, and income.

Some people object to what seems to them an abnor-
mal tendency of the elderly toward self-reflection and
reminiscing. Not so, writes Robert M. Butler in *Why Survive?* The kind of late-life storytelling my father was doing
about his war experiences was an important aspect of put-
ting his life in order and accepting his mortality and the
life cycle. For all older adults, it is important to reexamine
and reintegrate the various parts and pieces of life, especially those that involved unresolved conflict.

Some older adults are not totally aware of what they
are accomplishing by telling their story. Frequently their
stories are spontaneous and possibly unselective, rather
than deliberate. They seem subconsciously to know what
needs to be told, and they bring it to consciousness.

While conducting workshops in writing family stories,
I have discovered that most people have one story they
want to record. One older woman knew at once she wanted to preserve for her children the story of what happened
when she was a mother with three beautiful young daughters living on the farm.

One Easter morning she had dressed the girls in their
new pink dresses and off the family went to church. What
a lovely sight they were, like three flowers picked from the
same stalk. After church, as she was preparing the noon
meal, the girls went out to play in the yard. When she

called them for dinner, the youngest one did not respond. They searched the yard only to find her lying face down, the pink skirt extended, in the stock water trough. Now there were only two girls in pink dresses.

An older man told me the story of seeing dogs killing a bunch of turkeys. He and some friends had immediately told the owner so he could still butcher them. But he would always remember the sight of the dogs among the turkeys, rushing to and fro, slashing with their teeth.

Some older adults are able to retrieve material from their subconscious memory. One day when I was visiting Mother, she suddenly remembered that during the revolution she had stood on the back porch of the house to watch a group of people around an outdoor cauldron. During the famine people ate anything. These people had skinned a dog and were boiling it outside.

Another more mature student wrote an essay in a composition class about the auction sale held on her parents' farm following their sudden death in a car accident. The auctioneer, in a good-natured way, had put his hand on her shoulder and jokingly asked for bids on her. She couldn't believe his words and ran from him to the barn. Didn't he know she had just lost her parents? To her, his unthinking action was cruel.

This process of life review gives older adults, and sometimes younger ones, opportunity to decide what to do with the rest of their lives and to work out material and emotional legacies to children and friends. Possibly they may move on to do some creative work, such as writing their memoirs; painting or sketching; composing music; compiling family albums, scrapbooks, and genealogies. The forms of life review may be mild nostalgia ("It was wonderful to see the cows meander across the pasture to the barn"), mild regrets ("I never learned to skate"), or painful and severe recollections, as was the case with my father.

He wrote me a short letter in his retirement in which he briefly recalled a scene at the railroad station in Moscow when he and five young friends, not yet old enough to shave often but already in uniform, watched six train cars being loaded with young men for the front. "I saw how many parents, wives, sweethearts had come to say goodbye. They loaded at night, so not many would know what was going on. People wouldn't let go of each other. I cried too. Our Red Cross train followed them to the front [Dad was a Red Cross medic].

"I remember how we marched in Moscow. Nobody came to say goodbye to me. I remember how I stood all alone in Moscow, a country boy, wishing I could go home. Many of the young men got their cross, not of silver or gold to pin on their chest, but the wooden one in the graveyard in the 'brothers' grave, a mass grave without caskets."

Sharing one's life story is a natural healing process, a way of righting old wrongs, of dealing with guilt real and conditioned, of acknowledging accomplishments, of facing the life cycle and the fact that death sits in one corner. Story is a major way of giving unity and value to experience.

Story can become time-consuming, however, for the disinterested listener. I recall one time a large audience listened to a woman describe the 786 jars of fruit and vegetables she canned every year, the mountains of corn the family husked, the tins of cookies they baked, and what it was like to entertain fifty people at a meal. But it was important to her to recall what had been the essence of her life.

Stories have a special value. Walter Wangerin, Jr. explains that

> Whereas doctrine defines, finds boundaries, classifies and separates, story causes wholeness. Doctrine may engage the understanding and mind but story engages the human whole—body, senses, reason, emotion, memory, laughter, tears—so the one who has fragmented is put together again, and that under the governance of a new experience—the hearing of his own story told.

Wangerin also points out that story "knits people into a community whole, in time and across the times." That is what happens when Jews retell and relive the story of the exodus at Passover, when we hear the story of Moses and the thousands of frightened Israelites at the Red Sea with Egyptians in pursuit, when we retell the story of the cross at the Lord's Supper.

Wangerin writes,

> Peoples fragmented are put together again feelingly, in the very hearing of their common story told. This sort of wholeness is not a truth to be learned and preserved; it is itself experience, an event, which when God is believed to participate in it, becomes the Truth that preserves a people.

Our past—what happened back there—is sometimes the biggest hurdle to jump in growing older. I've met young people, bitter because of what happened in their homes, blaming parents, teachers, pastors. And I've met older adults who carry grudges because life wasn't fair. They stagger along, wondering why they're so loaded down.

I think Father felt more whole in the telling of his story about the war years. I hope so. And that is the essence of the gospel story—making people whole. There was probably much more Dad could have said, but it was enough for the time. I have told the story of his imprisonment to my children, and I hope they will tell it to theirs. Together, generation after generation, we will enter into the pain of people who war against one another and also destroy themselves in the process. And take steps to prevent it.

And to these stories I add my own of transition into aging, a transition as vital as graduating from college, marriage, death of a close relative. I do not apologize or belittle it. With these words I record that this border crossing is not a time of standing still, even though nothing of great dramatic quality seems to be happening.

Back there, in the past, are my stories, large and small —attending the university fifty miles away and eating a milkshake and a McDonald's hamburger (total of 50 cents) every day and listening to *Lara's Tune* in the student center on the jukebox while studying. Meanwhile, I agonized over what the children were doing at home alone, and why I had started what seemed like an impossible course of studies at my age. Then I reached that wonderful moment of graduation with a master's degree.

I remember rushing to Chicago to be at the bedside of Christine after a heart attack; I rode the subway in that complicated city, fearful of being mugged, but, even more, wondering whether I had taken the right train. I remember receiving a standing ovation for a speech; holding my first grandchild in my arms; seeing a book manuscript in print; going with the children on our first holiday after my husband's death . . . the list is endless.

I want my children to add their stories, small and large. My son James as a preschooler got lost in Macy's. Daughter Susan nearly drowned in a fast-flowing mountain stream in Glacier National Park and was rescued by a cousin in *Lederhosen*. As children James and Christine biked regularly to some older friends' farm to fish, carrying their lunch though they always knew they would also be invited to eat supper with this friendly older couple.

The grandchildren can begin their own saga. They can tell stories about spending a week with me each summer, and Christiana going on ride after ride on the most daring carnival rides until I was dizzy watching her, and her hiding from me one morning to tease me until I, thinking she had been abducted, started a major search for her.

One memory triggers another. Ira Proghoff writes in *At a Journal Workshop* that the soil of memory needs "to be tilled or it becomes hard-packed." Then it is no longer useful. And so I dig and dig.

13

How to stay alive: Laugh a little

Humor is an art of living; it keeps everything in its proper place.

In early 1990 I returned to Kansas from a visit to my mother and siblings in Alberta strangely rejuvenated. I hadn't expected that, because some family members had recently suffered severe health problems. I anticipated a down time, but I returned home bouyed by the family interchange.

It began innocently enough. All of us were sitting in my sister Anne's living room visiting, when some spark lit the kindling for humorous storytelling about the past. We couldn't quit, not until we had decided to compile a book of our stories to share with our children and with friends who had observed our experiences.

Anne loves telling the story of the time one of the local men in our small rural community and his girlfriend sang one of their popular duets, *Indian Love Call*, at a community function. This is a romantic song of a Native American warrior searching for his lost love as he paddles through a chain of lakes, soulfully pouring forth his adoration. He thinks he hears her echo his call and eagerly paddles to meet her. The two of them, who have continued to haunt the Qu'Appelle Lakes to this day, sing a duet. But it didn't work out quite that way. Anne writes,

> In this rendition, August's song started offstage. Then the lights came on and the audience saw water (a blue bunting banner stretched across the stage). Then from the left rear stage entered a tall brave, feather and all, paddling his canoe, which actually moved through (behind) the water. Toward the end of his song, he was joined in the canoe by the ghost of his sweetheart in full native dress. Their powerful duet rose to a stirring crescendo. Just as it reached its zenith, the blue bunting fell, and the audience saw a couple sitting in a tin bathtub being pulled by a rope. To add to the tension, the rope broke and the bathtub stopped in mid-stage. The lover continued to paddle (and sing). But he and his sweetheart weren't going anywhere. Finally, he had to get out of his conveyance and walk on "water" so he and the ghost could bring the song to its crowning finale.

The audience loved it and hollered their applause.

Anne told another story about the time she became the sacrificial lamb for a hair-curling experiment. Saturday was an important day for us Funk girls. We polished our shoes, darned our stockings, and washed and curled our hair. Curly hair, unless naturally curly, was either too expensive or unavailable.

But vanity always found a way. For a rinse, we girls used lemon juice on what we described as our mousy-blonde hair. We wanted it to look like Jean Harlow's. For setting gel, we boiled flax seed and water, then strained out the seeds and used the resulting heavy, industrial-strength glue to set our hair. It produced a helmet of wavy hair that could not be separated without an ax. Sometimes the waves were so big a ship could float in them, said Anne. But not to worry, we had waves. We were beautiful.

The daughter of a neighbor had graduated from the Marvel Hair Salon in the city but couldn't find a job. Mother decided we should give this would-be hairdresser some needed practice in giving cold permanent waves. Anne was chosen. I remember being terribly jealous that she would come back with curly hair and I would continue to have ugly, straight hair.

First the new hairdresser cut Anne's hair, then rolled it in curlers and doused it with solutions. She sat there—for hours—in anticipation of the raving beauty who would emerge. She was dreaming of hair like Little Orphan Annie's. But when she looked in the mirror after the rollers came out, her hair was straight as a board. And to make matters worse, the neighbor woman had cut it so short it couldn't be curled in the usual Saturday fashion. She was plain Jane—again!

Jack had all kinds of funny stories to add to the mix— often about his high school escapades, always more daring than stories we girls could produce. They included drinking gin with his friend before taking a steam bath, falling asleep on the bench in the bathhouse, and missing his party; or losing his clothes to the owner of the pond in which he and his friends were skinny dipping, a trespassing violation. They had to bargain with her, while discreetly holding hands over strategic places, to hoe her garden in exchange for their clothes.

Each of us had our own stories to share because each had had a different experience growing up in that small village with its wide variety of characters. I think we inherited our love of funny stories from our father. Noon during my childhood meant listening to Dad's stories about what had happened at the store, and Dad always saw the funny side of life in the early years.

One morning two women, both fairly stout (most Doukhobor women were overweight), wanted a private place to talk, so Dad said they could go into the passageway between the store and the warehouse. But the small corridor was dark. In their excitement about the news they were sharing, one woman backed the other woman to the end of the passageway. She stumbled and fell, head over heels, her voluminous skirts flapping, voice shrieking, down the stairs to the cellar and onto a pile of empty boxes at the bottom, which cushioned her fall. Dad never carried empty boxes to the basement; he always threw them.

Of course, the men in the store found this a very funny story, especially since the woman was not hurt. Their moral: that's what happens when women gossip.

But our stories as adults were frequently about Dad himself. I remember the Christmas Eve when he was still in the store after supper serving customers. Mother was preparing the turkey for Christmas and had emptied the roaster of the remains of the recent pork roast. She threw the rind, with its thick strip of fat, into the pot-bellied stove in the living room. We burned all trash. The rind exploded like a bomb and the fire rushed up the chimney, igniting the soot on its walls. Flames poured high out the chimney. I was convinced our house was burning down.

"Jack, run to the store and tell Dad to come home."

Off rushed my little brother with the news the house was burning.

"Tell Mom I can't come just now—too busy."

Back ran Jack with the message. The store always came first. Mother should have known. A chimney fire was her problem. His problem was looking after the store.

What to do? We children stood panicky. She didn't know how to put out fires and didn't know how to call the fire brigade. We had no telephone.

A passing drunk, already celebrating the season, stumbled into the house to tell us our chimney was burning. We knew that.

"Have you got some salt?"

Mother handed him the sack, which he poured onto the raging fire in the stove. It went out immediately. The Christmas preparations continued. And Dad continued serving customers at the store. The story is funny now, but it wasn't then.

Family strength through humor isn't accidental. It has to be nurtured. Part of our family's regular infusion of family spirit comes from a small newsletter published by my brother Jack. It includes news, stories, letters, and editorials only about our Funk family—no one else.

As Jack himself avows, he never lets mere facts get in the way of the truth he is reaching for. So he may stretch some facts to fit his case if trying to get his point across. Then when we siblings get together, we argue facts tenaciously. Was sister Anne born on top of a kitchen table behind the store in Rosenthal in south Russia, or where?

Mother insisted she wasn't. Jack insisted she was, so the table birth is debated again and again. We add more stories, some a little stretched, laugh a great deal, and provide new grist for Jack's mill.

Our supply of stories is inexhaustible. A word, an image, triggers a new sequence of images to uncover another buried treasure of truth. Daughter Christine remembers a trip she and I took with my sisters Anne and Frieda to Calgary to take an aunt to the airport. "All I can remember,"

Christine says, "is that we laughed the whole trip back." What we laughed about has long been forgotten. But it's a good memory for her.

When the following story about my sister Frieda and her husband, Henry, appeared in our family newspaper, I never questioned its authenticity. It had too many plausible "facts." Both had been born in the same village in south Russia. Then later Frieda and Henry met in Saskatchewan during World War II and married. That much I knew, but all the little details of when they actually first met escaped me. I knew that my parents had known Henry's parents in Russia and no more. Jack's account reads,

> Henry Schroeder, a little boy, four going on five, played under the big oak tree in Rosenthal, Ukraine, with some blocks his father had made for him. One block had a cross carved on one side. The boy was so engrossed in his play that he didn't notice the little girl with the reddish blonde hair watching him. She was about two, going on three. Henry carefully piled the blocks one on top of the other. The tower swayed precariously as it grew higher, but it held. Henry sat back to survey this magnificent structure he had built.
>
> Suddenly, without warning but with a squeal of delight, the little girl ran forward and kicked his carefully built tower. The blocks flew in all directions. Henry scrambled to pick up the blocks, but the little toddler grabbed the one with the cross and took it with her when her mother came to pick her up.
>
> Henry watched his block disappear in the grasp of the little girl, but she and her mother were soon lost in the crowd on their way to the railway station in Chortitza, where a large contingent of people were leaving for Canada.
>
> Three years later, it was Henry's turn with his family to get on a train and take the long trip to Canada. His blocks were forgotten. Henry and the little girl grew up in the

western Canadian provinces, met, fell in love, got married and raised a family.

Shortly after Henry and Frieda's marriage, Frieda's storekeeper father decided to move to Saskatoon. Henry and his new wife came to Blaine Lake to help arrange stuff for an auction sale. As they went through boxes of junk in the garage, Henry found a little wooden block with a cross on it. Faintly the memory of the blocks his father had made for him years ago in Russia flashed through his mind. At first he rejected the memory. It was just too much.

He took the block to his mother-in-law, who confirmed what he suspected. "Yes, that block came with us from Russia. I don't know where Frieda got it—but she had it on the train. She kept it and played with it a lot on the ship."

Henry took the block to his father. His father couldn't believe what he was seeing. Yes, he had made the block. He could only shake his head in wonder.

The next time I was in Edmonton I noticed a very old worn block with a cross on it in Henry and Frieda's china cabinet.

"Is this the block Jack mentioned in the Funk newsletter?"

"Yes, it is."

I examined it carefully. Why hadn't I heard about it before? It was certainly a very old child's block, worn by time. I didn't want to speak of the providence of God, but something strange had happened. Obviously blocks and marriages were made in heaven.

Then slowly rumors leaked out. We had been hoaxed by Henry and Jack. Jack had come to Henry one day and asked him to make him a child's block from weathered wood with a cross on it. Henry complied willingly. In fact, he made two, one for himself and one for Jack. And the plan was concocted to play on the gullibility of the family.

When the truth came out, for some time I refused to believe it. The story had been too carefully crafted. It provided such a romantic beginning for my sister's marriage nearly forty-five years earlier. Too many parts of the story were possible. But it wasn't true. Jack had the last word there. Now I am more wary.

But now I've got to decide whether the most recent newsletter announcement is true—that the story "The Block of Wood" won a prize at the recent convention of the Association of Family Newsletters held in Hawaii. The prize was a famous statuette known as the "The Tree" that looks a lot like the 500-year-old oak tree in Rosenthal where my parents once lived. Jack received the award by remote hookup.

I recognize anew the importance of humor as we grow older. It is possible to laugh despite severe losses. My brother has multiple sclerosis. Each of the other members have had severe health problems.

Much of being human is humorous. Out of difficult periods in life often comes a host of stories making light of troubles. Today we seek humor for humor's sake in stand-up comics, comic strips, and sitcoms. We tell anecdotes and jokes to get a few seconds of laughter, when we really need a humorous approach to our own life—an ability to see that the incongruities are cause for laughter, not for crying.

Jesus used humor to reveal truth, not merely to lighten a moment. If we read the Gospels with a freedom from presuppositions, we will see that Jesus laughed and expected others to laugh. But we're the serious ones, writes Elton Trueblood, and fear that the "acceptance of his obvious wit and humor would somehow be mildly blasphemous or sacrilegious. Religion, we think, is serious business, and serious business is incompatible with banter." My daughter Christine points out how the people in one congregation we attended were good people, but much too serious, too guilt-ridden, convinced that without them the world would fall apart.

For Trueblood, the strategy of laughter is more appropriate and effective than seriousness. He encourages laughter as the means to dissolve disappointment in others and similar experiences. "The recovery of laughter would be more than a relief; it would be a genuine social service." And many of us, especially older adults, have never laughed enough. Living alone, as many of us do, doesn't create enough opportunities to laugh with others.

During my father's final illness, I spent about ten days in Edmonton. Each day my sister Anne and I went to the hospital and sat by his bedside. He didn't always recognize us, nor could we converse much with him. His mind frequently wandered. The nurses had brushed his hair straight back, a style I had never seen on him. Each time I entered the room I wanted to change it at once so I saw the father I had known and loved rather than some stranger.

Each evening we returned home to relax on the couch and watch an episode on television of the newly released production of L. M. Montgomery's book *Anne of Green Gables* and laugh. We had grown up with this novel but now saw it through different eyes. I have pondered since our laughter over the strange antics of Anne, the young orphan who longed for a kindred spirit we had both learned to love in our childhood; I have realized it was relief from our pain.

Those older adults who laugh about their aging carry their age more lightly. Their repertoire of topics includes their physical infirmities, longevity, forgetfulness, money or lack of it, retirement problems, reluctance to tell their age, relationship to children and grandchildren, and even deaths and funerals. But I hope family stories dominate.

So I liked the story below, by Anne, that appeared in the next issue of the Funk newsletter after our marathon storytelling. It attempts to understand the present by making use of the past in a humorous way. What our stories are about isn't as important as the spirit in which they are told. The stories we siblings tell show me the spirit that makes us a family. Mother, at age ninety-eight, didn't always catch our humor, but listened good-naturedly. After all, she knew the truth about where Anne was born—and it wasn't on the kitchen table. We want our family to be a strong family, for we may yet have many more difficult experiences to endure as we all get even older. Laughter greases the way. And keeps us alive.

Anne's story hints at that spirit of family unity. It begins with the epigram, "We were first, and boldly went where no man had gone before." She writes,

The Funk girls in Blaine Lake were the original Star Trekkers—except we didn't get any recognition like those Johnny-come-latelys, the NASA astronauts.

Our little playhouse, the shed behind the garage, was our spaceship. The control panel was near the door, and before the spaceship was put into orbit, the door was securely locked and no one—but no one—was allowed to leave. Mother didn't understand why we needed supplies for a year, but with or without the buns and crumb cake, we went on our year-long cruise.

Frieda was the captain, of course, and decided where we would go and how long we would stay. Because she was studying Esperanto, the international language, under the tutelage of a local immigrant from Europe who was convinced that this would be the world language of the future, she gave us daily lessons in a special language we created called Differene. We knew we would need it if we met other space travelers.

We traveled to Mars, Venus, and beyond our solar system to the stars. A trip to the moon was a short but exciting trip. We saw the craters on the moon long before Buzz Aldrin did. A trip to the sun took longer. We had to be careful we were not burned.

Eventually we had to return to earth and face its mundane routines. Now I am bored when I see Star Trek on TV. I've been there.

As I read Anne's story, I recall my intense longing to be at the control panel by the door, but I was a middle child and only older children had that privilege. In my imagination I see us Funk girls, arms symbolically interlocked, boldly facing the Depression world using the weapon of our imagination. Nothing could daunt or harm us when we were free to imagine.

My prayer for each sister and my brother as we all move toward age seventy and beyond it is that we will face this period of time in the same way—boldly, creatively, with faith—and with humor.

Someone has said, "No fortress is as strong as the common life." When I left for home after that trip, I felt that for a few days I had celebrated that common life with humor. I could face what lay ahead a little better.

14

Making the fairies last

After a while I find I've lost
the green-jerkined goblins who fiercely fought
to climb the light cord near my bed
and plummet topspeed on my head.

After long years I can't recall
if Goldilocks and Midas met,
if three little pigs ran to the mill,
or if Miss Muffet danced on a hill.

I wonder if cockle bells cockled
or cackled like farm hens who haggled
about whose Little Chick went round and round
convinced the sky was falling down.

Did Jack-in-the-pulpit preach and pray
to mice—or bees—at edge of day?
The years, the elves, fly past too fast;
how can I make the fairies last?—KFW

I have watched from a distance my sister Anne's growing interest in and involvement with painting following her retirement from teaching. She tells me there is little she looks forward to as much as her painting class. She loses herself in her painting when she retires to her basement studio and shuts the door.

She is not alone in finding a late-life avenue of expression in the creative arts. Elder hostels, Shepherd's Centers, Free Universities, and continuing education and enrichment classes for older adults offer a wide variety of opportunities to pick up interests of their youth, or sometimes to begin something brand new.

Some older adults blame their failure to become involved in new creative pursuits and to produce on lack of physical energy, not on lack of talent. Yet, writes John A. B. McNeil in *The Ulyssean Adult*, the greatest factor that keeps older adults from remaining creative is not lack of physical energy, but lack of psychic energy. A person may become locked into unchangeable patterns of living. The question McNeil asks, and which I have asked myself, is how can an older adult break free from increasing "physical inertia, psychic despair, and the failure of nerve and confidence?" I've experienced it. The fairies don't last.

Erik Erikson writes in *Vital Involvement in Old Age* that older adults may have had little preparation in early life for aging. It then becomes hard to push ahead in the creative arts, a field which they had never seriously considered before. Now that older adults have the time, they think they have no creative ability, which Erikson believes may be the result of cultural conditioning. Many are limited in social contacts to their peer group, a group not given to encouraging risk by creating in new modes. Sensory experiences as stimuli to new thought may be limited to going to church, listening to the radio, watching television, and eating out. Exposure to drama, theater, and art becomes less and less.

So it isn't unusual to hear an older adult say, "It's not

for me. I'd be out of my depth" when they see what people such as Verdi, Michelangelo, Picasso, and Rembrandt have done. But here's comfort from Alex Comfort (*A Good Age*) who writes that it's not best to look at the continuous creativity of such outstanding people for inspiration. Their creative expression usually began when they were young and simply continued. Late-life creativity, as I am thinking of it here, is an activity begun when one has laid down one's former work.

I have found that older adults can be very creative when given the opportunity. About fifteen years ago, the director of the life enrichment class at the college where I was teaching asked if I would consider teaching writing to this group. How many students might I expect? About nine or ten. The first day of class I had twenty-nine older men and women and more kept coming.

Since my rule has always been to try to get students to write about what they know the most about, I suggested they write about their personal experiences. They wrote and wrote. From that class developed my book *Good Times with Old Times: How to Write Your Memoirs* (Herald Press). One woman went on to self-publish her memoirs, a delightful account of growing up during the Depression in a family with ten siblings.

I started this book as a challenge to myself. I was seriously thinking about ending my writing career. I only knew the beginning of this book when I started, and even that was perplexity and frustration. I didn't know the end. What if it also was perplexity and frustration? I had found myself writing things in my journal that disturbed me as I contemplated retiring from teaching and turning to something else despite the exuberant comments from new retirees, "I just love retirement." New retirees are walking, traveling, dining out. But what happens when one or the other becomes unable to keep up?

A local Women in the Arts project encouraged residents of nursing homes to express themselves on paper about growing old. "Aging is gray," they said. "It sounds like a bunch of cats in a gunny sack. . . . It smells like bleach and tastes like medicine," "Aging is light blue. It sounds like mama in the kitchen. . . . It tastes like ice cream." Does creativity help us choose the color we are painting life?

It became clear to me that this period in my life was soil that also needed to be tilled or it would become hard-packed. I had to make the border-crossing experience, which I soon saw to be a major transition, accessible to myself and not give up creativity. Either I controlled the direction my life was taking or I might end up like my father—withdrawn, distressed, wondering where the joy of life had gone.

Ira Proghoff in *At a Journal Workshop* points out that the metaphor Dag Hammarskjold used in his autobiographical book, *Markings*, was natural to him, a lifelong mountain climber. Just as a climber leaves markings behind as he proceeds up the mountain, so Hammarskjold recorded his climb up and down the mountain of his life. It was the record of his path through life, his attempt to find the path through the maze.

The transition I was going through was as vital as graduation from a university, marriage, birth of a child, or death of a close relative. Why not trace my passage also? I was determined to be as honest with myself as possible. I wouldn't censor or falsify for the sake of the story. I wouldn't apologize or explain away what was happening or not happening, even though I didn't like to admit to discomfort—and some loneliness.

I was keenly aware of roads I might take—continue teaching for a few more years, accept the co-pastorate of a small congregation in the city (as I had often dreamed of doing), make writing my main activity, travel, speak, work in the area of older adult ministries in the church, become more involved in volunteer ministries, or drop all activity and warm my couch. These unlived experiences stood before me. Which did I have the courage and inner urging to pursue?

McNeil offers three encouragements to those who stand at such crossroads. The first is to accept the "sacred present'" (Alfred North Whitehead's term). For McNeil this means not to

> mourn the past fruitlessly, not to sit chilled and immobilized by thoughts of how one is situated on entering the last years of life, but rather to greet the day lovingly, and to live its precious hours as though yesterday's sorrows and tomorrow's hazards were what they mostly are—chimeras luring us from the sweet airs and the beautiful road of the day-by-day actualization of our self.

I had to let go of college teaching as I once knew it, much as I had enjoyed it. It belonged to a new group of educators. Students had changed, administrators and colleagues had changed, curriculum was changing. I couldn't throw away my teaching files the first year, but each successive year I was able to toss out another box or two, often gladly, occasionally mad with delight. I still cling to a few files of classes I enjoyed very much, especially those I can use in Bible teaching.

McNeil's second encouragement is to recognize your potentiality and not to give in to the myths and stereotypes of aging. I recall the story about the little engine who, when faced with climbing the mountain, kept repeating to himself, "I think I can, I think I can," and before he knew it he was over the hill. But what if you haven't done anything for decades and your mind is rusty with disuse and your emotions in disorder?

Begin where you are, advises McNeil, in a "relaxed mood of friendship" with yourself and engage in some simple action. This first activity doesn't need to turn out successful, but it is a beginning in "exploration, probing, tuning in and testing, the cat marks of curiosity."

The twelve to eighteen months after I no longer went to school to teach classes each morning, I capitulated to current thinking that retirees are has-beens, fit only for the trashbin of life. I moped around, fearing the emptiness of the next day. But I perked up again and again whenever I met someone ten or more years older who showed vital interest in life and was still growing and moving ahead. I noted with interest the man who was still driving at seventy-eight, the woman who was still traveling at nearly eighty, and the woman who was still writing thought-provoking books at eighty-five. There was life after sixty-five. I didn't need to quit writing and studying.

McNeil also recommends various activities to keep the mind agile. Improve your vocabulary by working cross-word puzzles. Keep a dictionary handy (I have one in each of three rooms so it takes little effort to find one). Take a class. (I took a few short courses first and then audited another seminary course.) Keep up with the language of the day. Reject slang and religious clichés you picked up forty years ago. Try out new uses of language. Read. Watch quiz shows. Question.

Do a routine job differently, he suggests. If you always

walk a certain path, try a new one. Put a quota on "the de-
structive indulgence of sad drifting of thoughts, of nostalgic sorrow for the dear dead days beyond recall, and of resigned passivity and refuge in the routine." Later on, when
you are the old-old, there will be much time for contem-
plation.

Clap your hands for someone else—for children,
grandchildren, other older people. Become a cheerleader
for someone. Go to performances you know won't be
well-attended. Learn humor. Keep a joke handy. If you
flub the telling, try again.

I have an older friend who told us this one. An old man
found a frog who said to him, "Kiss me on my lips and I'll
turn into a beautiful young lady."

The old man picked up the frog and put it in his pocket.

"Hey, I thought I told you to kiss me on my lips and I'd
turn into a beautiful young lady," cried the frog.

"At this point in life, I'd rather have a talking frog," re-
plied the man.

I caution myself, as a former English professor, to be
less critical of other people's grammar, even if it's only an
inner comment to myself wishing I didn't have to listen to
people abusing the English language. So I hear "drug"
used as the past tense of "to drag" or "I" used for the objec-
tive case. What difference will it make in the final analysis?
What would I do if in glory I met Saint Peter and he said,
"Between you and I . . ."? Some academic and political
leaders don't know the difference between these usages.
All are just forms of linguistic etiquette. I understand the
person speaking, so what concerns me?

A third recommendation McNeil has for people ready
to yield to the inertia that keeps them from creativity is to

realign their lives. McNeil suggests turning from being an "eternal receiver, the droning echoer (which so many older adults become)" to being the active questioner, "the zestful attacker of hundreds of riddles which life delivers to us if we are alive to them."

In essence, he recommends making a career out of being old. That means risking a new activity, a new idea. The creative person has less need to make self and world stable. This means catching your mind when you find yourself clamping down on an opinion, whether it is related to young people, music, cars, sex, worship or politics. Remain open to affirm and receive.

I urge older adults to reject organizations that indulge in the lowest common denominator of being old if that style doesn't agree with them, and to turn to other forms of recreative entertainment. I reject table games at ten in the morning and bingo at ten at night as a matter of habit. Look for a group in which you are free to be yourself—to be absurd, outrageous on occasion—not to have to watch what you say for fear your words will be taken out of context, I tell them. Avoid getting enmeshed in institutions and organizations that strangle growth.

After testing a few volunteer activities, I selected hospice as one way I intended to volunteer my time and energy. Hospice volunteer work has not brought me close friends but has taken me into a wide range of homes and experiences, all related to death and dying.

I have also begun volunteer work at a nonprofit gift shop that markets crafts made by artisans of poor countries to ensure them a better livelihood. By that move I place myself on the side of the poor, if only in a small way.

I plan to tackle the mountain of material I have collected about my family's past in Russia and turn it into something worth leaving behind. Perhaps a novel? Do I dare risk?

When I determined to move more into older adult ministries, it came as no surprise when the then executive secretary of Mennonite Health Association asked me to edit/write the book *Life After Fifty: A Positive Look at Aging in the Faith Community* (Faith & Life Press). A slim volume of prayers about the transitions of aging, *Prayers of an Omega: Facing the Transitions of Aging* (Herald Press), followed. This book is another effort to gain better understanding of this stage of development.

In my congregation I joined the older adult ministries team. Movement is slow but happening, for we're aware that the baby boomer generation is knocking at the door. If I don't like what's happening, I tell myself, I am free to criticize only if I work at improvement. I don't want to stay benched. Volunteering takes me off the bench.

I recall an older player in the game of life who never stayed "benched." I met Aggie Klassen in 1977. A youth periodical asked me to interview her for their paper. "Where can we go to talk?" I asked when she met me on the ground floor one cold blustery day in January at the Voluntary Service house in Wichita where she lived.

"Oh, up in my pad."

I gulped. Pad? The word didn't quite fit my image of a mature Voluntary Service worker, which her gray hair told me she was. Her pad felt comfy despite the bitter cold weather. Later, when Aggie told me about an event in her life that had scared her "spitless," I knew I wasn't talking to the ordinary volunteer.

Like some of her unofficially adopted "sons" in the state penitentiary doing life for murder, she was in voluntary service for life. She was a full-fledged, card-carrying

VSer with one difference—her contract had no term of service written in. And what kept her in was love, not bars. Voluntary service was more than a way of spending time while trying to find out what you want to do with your life. To her, it was a way of life.

After her husband's death and the realization he was not coming back again—ever, she told herself firmly, "You've got to get involved with people or you will go batty thinking only about yourself and your needs." She began to step out.

She joined a black church. Friends, family, neighbors, black pastors, and white pastors wondered if she had to go that far to be true to her ideals. "That will be a good mission field for you," suggested a member of her former church. But that wasn't Aggie's plan. She wasn't there to tell the blacks how to do things better. "I learned a lot about their problems and found out how their minds ticked and how we whites looked to them."

Her probing mind took her in another direction. She was accepted on the visiting list of a young black prisoner at the state industrial reformatory. She had known this prisoner as a student several years earlier, when she worked as a school librarian. He was in for murder and drug charges. Then she was accepted on the visiting lists of three other prisons, an unusual arrangement when prison regulations state that one person should visit only one prisoner regularly.

From there she became a short-term VSer to work on completing a church survey. Next came long-term Voluntary Service and becoming a member of an intentional community in Wichita. When she sold her home in Newton, one person told her, "You have sold your security down the river and burnt all the bridges."

But Aggie didn't agree. "What do I want with money? I have security here. I know I will never be left alone. We will always stick together and take care of each other. I have become convinced that community is the biggest way of growing spiritually."

She told one group, "I started late in learning about love, but you have your life before you." The Voluntary Service director at the time told me that he thought her charisma came from her prayer life. "She's either highly intuitive or she speaks to God." She celebrated her seventieth birthday that month.

I had always thought of volunteer work as something someone did to help a professional do his or her job—stuff envelopes, carry flowers, shelve library books, and distribute mail to patients. Yet Aggie was a great example of what leaders of some older adult ministries recommend—that older adults be free to use their creativity and even management skills in volunteer work, not just to do repetitive work that is an extension of the arms and legs of the planner of the project.

Any positive view of the elderly is subtly being leeched by broad generalizations that all older adults are mindless human husks. The term *senile* is a term of abuse if applied to an entire generation of the elderly. Only about one percent of older people are or can expect to become senile, or to be affected by Alzheimer's disease. The condition of senility in older age is not general, yet because such persons are brought together in visible heaps in nursing homes, society labels all elderly by that term. The result is great loss of respect for the "hoar head," and consequently the young-old resist growing older.

In *The Mature Mind*, first published in 1949, Harry Overstreet writes that society at the time was glamorizing youth because the image of adulthood did not inspire. Youth looked at adults around them falling into a dreary procession of years filled with routine and boring work. Adulthood had no intrinsic dignity and worth. No challenge. Overstreet quotes William Sheldon as saying the image of adulthood was "smug, vulgar, and deadening."

In the 1960s and 1970s, youth resisted growing up because the image and symbols of adulthood lacked appeal. Adulthood was not seen as a time of increasing power and fulfillment, only as a letting go, making the best of a boring bargain. After the free joyous years of youth were over, you endured life. Now youth are falling from the pedestal and the middle adult is on the throne. The people at the other end, the older adults, are looking for a place to stand.

During the late 1950s, J. D. Salinger wrote the best-seller *The Catcher in the Rye*. Young people bought several million copies and devoured the contents. Adults found the book decidedly dull. In it, fifteen-year-old Holden Caulfield, a high school flunkout, takes a close look at the adults in his life—teachers, parents, administrators, friends—and rejects them all as phonies. He wonders what will happen to all the girls he knows. He deplores that they will probably marry "dopey guys" who always talk about how many miles they get to a gallon in their cars, guys that get sore and childish if you beat them at golf or Ping-Pong, guys that never read books, guys that are boring. These vacant symbols of adulthood disgust him.

His life's ambition is to find some way to keep the children playing in the rye field from falling over the cliff into adulthood. He wants to catch them so they remain forever young.

Though Holden's view of adulthood may not be accurate, this unenticing portrait of grownup life spawned the generation gap and the resulting hippie movement and student riots of the late sixties. Young adults singled out a weakness in adult life—it did not inspire. For several decades older adults have been accused of the same weakness—old age does not inspire.

Now the pendulum is changing. A new image is emerging of older adulthood as creative and fulfilling. The new challenge is to become a learner for life. The way to stay alive is to accept that God can invade a life and set that person on a meaningful course of discipleship at every age. The adventure of growth is possible at any time. Youth and adults have no monopoly here. This book is a record of my journey to that position.

And it becomes clearer to me: I want to be a catcher in the rye for older adults before they fall off the cliff and think of themselves as nobodies. I want them to keep growing. And to help me grow.

15

Funerals are opportunities

Why is it that we rejoice at a birth and grieve at a funeral? It is because we are not the person involved. —Mark Twain

Two tasks expected of those who discontinue full-time employment are making noodle casseroles for church suppers and attending funerals. My elderly neighbor and I used to joke that she spent her time going to funerals and I to meetings. Now I too attend funerals.

And it's not an entirely unpleasant task, especially if the deceased enjoyed a good long life and a good death. Everyone deserves the dignity of a good death, not a prolonged one extended needlessly by tubes, needles, catheters, and respirators hooked to every orifice. To die at home surrounded by a loving family and faithful friends is a rare privilege, although hospice organizations are increasingly working to make this an option.

Funerals are good places for thinking. I review my memories of the one who died, especially the times when our lives touched. And I grieve with the family and friends because they cannot add new memories to their store through continued relationships with the deceased. Then maybe they're glad the relationship is over. Who knows? I wonder about that too.

Visiting an older parent becomes a tremendous burden to some children. What can you talk about with a deaf father who keeps telling the same boring stories over and over again? You heard them yesterday, you heard them last week, and you know you'll hear them again next week. Why doesn't he tell some new ones? I rejoice when an elderly sick parent has been released from long suffering and from the need to tell the same stories over and over, because no new ones are being added to his experience and the mind has lost the memory file of recent ones.

I think about other funerals I have attended. I think of the time my husband died seven weeks after we had moved to a new community. I pictured myself and my children huddled desolate in one pew and a few friends on another as in an old English Victorian novel. When I walked into the sanctuary and saw it filled with encouragers, all strangers to me, including the children's school classes, I felt overwhelmed. I was not alone after all. God's eagle wings were supporting me and my children.

Obituaries and the sharing of memories by family and friends are also interesting to listen to, especially if they're more than a string of biographical facts. A funeral is the great straightening-out day for those who don't know who belongs to whom. If those two people in the front row were sisters or brothers, how come it never showed? A funeral is a great occasion to sort out family members and get everyone sitting on the right branch of the family tree.

Sometimes I have great fun wondering what the deceased included in the will. Are the mourners waiting anxiously for it to be read?

I suggest we add another kind of will—a spiritual one —to be read publicly. Before Moses died, he gathered his sons to his bedside and blessed each according to the son's nature. He gave each a spiritual legacy. Our concern these days is the legal distribution of material possessions– land, money, investments, family heirlooms, library, files. To assess spiritual gifts and distribute them is equally important. I ask myself how I want my children and grand-children to remember me. What do I have to give away? Who needs this spiritual trust fund to begin or continue life?

Sometimes, while I sit, I plan my own funeral. I ask my-self questions. How would I like my funeral conducted? Where? By whom? Memorials? And there's the matter of the coffin. I prefer plain wooden coffins to the ornate bronze ones. What is the importance of being preserved from the dust-to-dust process as long as possible? Yet wooden coffins aren't easily obtained because they aren't assembly-line products. A congregation-owned pall to cover every coffin would equalize every burial box from the most elaborate to the lowly cloth-covered one.

What about pallbearers? I read the funeral folder care-fully to note their names and try to figure out their rela-tionship to the deceased. Wedding folders are more ex-plicit about relatives. At a funeral you're left in the dark or forced to nudge your neighbor for an answer. Nowadays daughters and granddaughters are included in the list of pallbearers. That's probably because no one "bears" any-thing. The funeral directors wheel the casket in and out with a touch of the hand. Pallbearers don't even always walk beside the casket. I wish they would.

On a visit to India a number of years ago, our party ar-rived just after the sudden death of the infant daughter of a national seminary student couple. With missionary friends, I visited the home late that same day. The tiny child was laid out on the white bed strewn with bright flowers. She looked like a fragile flower cut too soon. Family and friends planned to spend the night singing hymns and drinking tea.

At the funeral service early the next morning, we were told this was the third time little Hannah was at the altar, once at her dedication, a second time at Christmas when she played the role of the baby Jesus, and now at her death. My clearest image of the entire event is the sight of the tiny coffin being carried by pallbearers half a mile to the cemetery with the congregation following, singing. These pallbearers felt the pain of their friends' burden, literally and figuratively.

I enjoy flowers at a funeral, not that banks of them are important. Sometimes I wonder whether the deceased received even one bouquet a year for the last ten years. When traveling in the former Soviet Union, I noticed that flowers are much more important to the daily life of those people than they are to us. It was not uncommon to see workers purchase a bouquet on the way home from work. I tried to imagine them greeting a waiting wife, maybe a mother or father or a friend at home. Vendors stood at street corners, urging us to buy.

Where would I like to be buried? While in the former Soviet Union, I visited a graveyard in the village where my father was born and spent some of his adult life. As I examined old broken gravestones with German inscriptions, I reminded myself that in the winter of 1919-20, during the revolution, my father, as a young man, had buried four close relatives within a period of two weeks in this very same graveyard: father, grandfather and grandmother, and uncle. They had all died of typhus. He alone had been the undertaker responsible for washing and preparing the bodies, for building a coffin out of fence slats, he alone was in charge of getting the bodies to the cemetery, in charge of praying over them and closing the grave. That experience never left him. It was a lonely, gut-wrenching experience.

We don't wail and tear our clothes as in some cultures to show grief. We are more sophisticated than the Middle-eastern people I saw in a waiting room of a Chicago hospital who wailed and threw themselves about. We stand calm, controlled, maybe sniffle a bit. "She's really taking it well," we assure ourselves after a funeral as we discuss the new widow's emotional state. That means we won't have as much comforting work to do. We like people who show strength, who don't mess up our lives or shirt collars by getting weepy.

Yet even if we don't allow mourners to wail openly, I hope they get a chance to wail privately and together. To lament, to cry before God, is a necessary stage in suffering for healing to take place.

I recall one funeral many years ago at which the new widow stood up and gave a glowing testimony of how wonderfully God was taking care of her every need. Why did she feel it necessary to mute her pain? To be superhuman? If praise is only a pumped-up effort, and I hope hers wasn't, it can become stilted and mechanical because it does not come from an encounter with God, but is a "thing to do" when Christians are together. I have wondered what happened when the reality of being alone set in for that woman. The move to acceptance of the death, to solidarity with God's will, to the conquest of powerlessness, to praise, comes later. It does not exclude sorrowing.

Persons have shared with me from time to time how hard it is to find someone who will allow them to grieve, or lament, openly, without passing judgment on them or shutting them up with "cheer-up" words: "God will be with you; it's going to be okay. Ruthie may have died, but you can always have another child," "This death of your husband is the Lord's will for you." The comforter's intentions are good, but the words are not freeing. In response, the sufferer moves the hurt deeper inside.

To suffer at all is painful; to suffer alone is agony. To tell the sufferer that to have strong feelings is wrong hinders healing. Before a sore can heal, the pus must ooze out. Before a person can be spiritually healed, the anger, hurt, frustration, and sense of loss must be released. To share pain is to be freed from the terror of the loneliness accompanying the pain and suffering.

In pioneer days women created grief quilts for husbands, for children, and for themselves, out of the fabrics of their lives. A grieving mother made a quilt with patches from all the clothing of a now-dead daughter. In the quilt, the mother could review her daughter's life. Attending a funeral is piecing a quilt out of memories of the deceased's life.

At my husband's funeral, an older woman, a complete stranger, took my hand in hers and said simply, "It won't always be like this." With those few words she acknowledged my pain and gave me hope. To this day I don't know her name. Her face, but not her words, became blurred, because of the many strangers I met that day. So at a funeral I look for an opportunity to pass on hope.

Clearly, funerals in our culture are not children's activities unless a close relative is being buried. Yet death, like life, belongs to children, especially in this violent age. Why do we protect children from all experiences with death? Some will experience a parent's or a sibling's death much too soon.

Will the time ever come when cremation will become more common than burial? With growing populations I think it will. In India we watched from behind hidden windows at the river Ganges as the men brought the prepared corpses on litters into the area where they would be cremated. The eldest son anointed the body with *ghee* and lit the match.

I have never known all the reasoning behind my mother's decision to have my father's body cremated after the public viewing. This woman, who was often concerned about what other people would think, went against prevailing sentiment in the Christian church that bodies should be buried when she asked for cremation. After discussing cremation with each of us children from every standpoint, including the biblical ones (people burned to death in a house or lost at sea will surely be present at the great resurrection even if their bodies were destroyed here), she decided on cremation. Father's urn of ashes was buried under a tree at my brother's home. She wanted her ashes to be buried there also. And they were. But I think part of her decision was influenced by the fact that her parents and most of her siblings lie in some unknown grave; some of them perished after World War II in difficult circumstances of starvation, privation, and the violence of war. Why should her body receive better treatment? Or was it that the thought of her body being buried in a vast city cemetery felt too impersonal? I don't know.

Sometimes I let my own questions about life and death float to the top. God has the answer to all our problems, says the preacher. Why then doesn't God heal my daughter's illness, chronic and sometimes life-threatening? Why do I have to live alone year after year?

Life has its burdens, I tell myself. There is the burden of life itself, especially for older adults who can find little reason to keep on living. There is the burden of decreasing health and strength. We fear infirmity and dependence. Suicide is a leading cause of death among the frail elderly, especially older men. Being human means pain, suffering, disease, disability, aging, and death. So we idolize technology and turn to it and to government agencies as the lifter of life's burdens. But the answer doesn't lie there.

There is the burden of sin. Though the atmosphere presses down on us at the rate of several pounds per square inch, we are not conscious of this weight, but we are conscious of the weight of sin. A harsh word, a wrongful betrayal, an unforgiving spirit—each is heavier than a sledgehammer.

There is the burden of responsibility for others while we are alive and also after we die of the memories people will have of us. Parents who have handicapped children worry about who will care for them after the parents are gone.

There is the burden of life work. Sometimes life ends before the task one has set for oneself is complete.

All of us have as much hill-climbing, burden-bearing, as we can manage. I can't carry the burden of your life, your sin, your responsibility for others. But God steps in and bears us and our burden. This person whose homegoing we are commemorating at the funeral is free of all burdens. I praise God.

A funeral is also an opportunity to think about my own mortality. "All flesh is as grass," wrote Isaiah. I recently attended the funeral of an older friend in a congregation we once belonged to. We human beings have no dominion over time, I told myself, as I observed these former friends, now graying, some stooped and walking slowly, mourning the loss of a friend.

In past centuries a favorite subject for poets was death, for it was always very near. Sex was a dirty word, hidden under the covers. Life then was short, tenuous at best, threatened by disease, daily violence, and natural disasters. Today sex is the main topic of discourse, and death is the dirty word. Instead of getting rid of guilt, we get rid of our clothes. Death is an indication of our finiteness, the necessity of giving up good things, of ending up in a powerless situation. Sex today symbolizes strength and power, and the experience of it seems close to feeling infinite for some.

One of the leading magazines for older adults doesn't let thoughts of death sneak in. Advertisements in this periodical are never for items that signify life is moving toward an end—no wheelchairs, canes, walkers, incontinence pads, wrinkle cream, prostheses, medications for constipation or other ills. Instead I find advertisements for travel opportunities, automobiles, investments, health foods, leisure clothes, and medication for minor ailments. Death is nowhere in sight.

One of the best short stories that depicts the power of death is Yuri Olesha's "Lyompa." At first the disappearance of things the sick man values do not particularly sadden him. Then the possibility of migrating to America leaves him, next of being handsome, rich, having a family (he is single). In a single day he is abandoned by the street, his job, the mail, horses. Little by little his coat, the door key, his shoes all lose all significance. "Death was destroying things on its way to him." Instead he has things forced on him he doesn't want: frightening visits and looks of people he knows. His greatest loss is the right to choose.

I don't expect people today to yearn for death like some early martyrs who looked forward to a horrible death as the greatest spiritual ecstasy possible. Fear of suffering and death is instinctive. Death is part of the natural, created order. What happens at death is impenetrable. The ancient preacher wrote: "He has also set eternity in the hearts of men; yet they cannot fathom what God has from beginning to end" (Eccles. 3:11). In other words, to be human is to bear knowledge that is too big for us. Animals are not like this. We know we will die. They don't. No, this death reminds me that God has given us life; we should live fully until we die. God is on the side of life and health. God is not abandoning the world when someone dies.

So I think about what comes next—after death. A funeral reminds us that we are citizens of two worlds. The one is the world of noise and work, silence and easy chairs, travel and waiting, hope and frustration, rewards and disappointments. Then there is the other world, the endless one beyond this one, to which we all must go some day. No one will escape life after death. It is our human destiny.

That's why I like the old hymns of heaven sung mostly at funerals; their simple orthodoxy is comforting. They acknowledge freely, openly, that the faith life for the individual and for the church is leading somewhere—to a glorious union with our Creator. "For me to live is Christ, to die is gain," wrote the apostle Paul. Our faith teaches us that our encounter with this fearless intruder moves us ahead in our history with our Lord.

I recall the sudden death of my older friend Hannah Willems and how we became friends. One day in church shortly after we had moved to Hillsboro, a friend said,

"Here's someone you should meet." Hannah Willems was walking down the aisle, confidently, with a warm open smile. After that, little by little, we as a family moved into the lives of her and her husband, Peter B. They lived across the railroad track from us, and many an evening we sat around their table eating peppermint ice cream and cookies, and drinking tea.

At times the relationship was close, at other times further apart because of our own circumstances, yet as a family we knew the Willemses were there if we needed them. If I had some achievement I had to tell someone about, I could always call her. If I needed a shoulder to weep on for a while, she was ready with hers. If the children had a sudden problem, they knew where to go.

She died suddenly in surgery. The evening before the funeral, I visited the funeral home. I'm not quite sure why I went. I am not much given to viewing "remains." Perhaps I wanted to assure myself someone hadn't made up the story about her death. But there she lay in her favorite navy-blue dress with white polka-dot collar. Her hands were calmly folded, very unlike the way I had learned to know her. Her hands were usually busy making meals for others, writing letters, or helping in some way.

How often had we eaten meals prepared by those hands? She had a gift for hospitality, knowing when people were lonely and alone. She did not believe in taking turns. Her turn often came two or three times in succession.

As I stood at her open coffin, I wondered who would take her place in praying for us. She often told me she believed in prayer. She shared answers to prayer with me. If I told her a problem, her first response was usually, "We will pray for you."

Persons who are forced to accept gifts from others, as we were during our early years as a single-parent family in Hillsboro, sometimes wonder whether the giving is charity performed out of a sense of duty or love for one's own sake. Her frequent words, "We need you, Katie, as much as you need us," erased all suggestions that she might be trying to add a few stars to her crown.

And so I lay a spray of flowers in Hannah Willems' memory as I participate in other funerals because of what she meant to me and my family. And at a funeral I hold hands with all who knew the deceased and share their grief for a while.

Some people have many experiences with death. Others only a few. Some people wait for death of a sick loved one a long time. Others face it suddenly. "Fear is a long journey; sorrow at least an arriving," says the elder priest to Pastor Kumalo in Alan Paton's *Cry, the Beloved Country*. Kumalo has lived with fear for many weeks out of concern for his wayward son. When the word arrived that his son had been apprehended by the police for a criminal act, the time for sorrow has come. The young man is later executed for his part in a murder.

Death is always a signal that sorrowing must begin. Another stage in the journey can begin. But even sorrow will not be without end. God has set limits to day and night, winter and summer. God is in control and will bring comfort. And above all, we have the knowledge of eternity in our hearts.

16

Teacher, how many words do I need for tomorrow's essay?

Let us not become weary in doing good, for at the proper time we will reap a harvest if we do not give up. Gal. 6:9

My task for twenty-four years was to teach students to use words. I assigned essays. Invariably, after I had given the assignment, a student would raise a hand, "Mrs. Wiebe, how long does this paper have to be? How many words do I need for tomorrow's essay?"

In other words, "Tell me when I have satisfied you—when I have churned out enough words to make you happy."

I would look at the student. All the others were waiting for an answer also. He or she was only a spokesperson for them. "Tell us when we can quit," some expressions said. The length of the essay was an important matter to them. Fewer words meant more time for watching TV, drinking cokes in the Student Center, or wandering the campus in search of excitement. If I said, "As many words as necessary to complete the assignment you set for yourself," I'd hear a groan.

So I'd say, "Two or three typewritten pages—double-spaced—or about 500 words"—or some other figure.

And then I'd wait for the papers.

I always enjoyed reading student papers that showed original thought. After the papers had been handed in, I would sort them first—typed papers with clear dark print on the top of the pile, then those in which the print was less legible because of a worn-out ribbon on typewriter or printer (some print was so pale it looked like ghost-writing), then neatly handwritten ones (always a few), and then finally the papers that would take patience and courage to figure out (red or green ink, pencil, or some code developed for an alien enemy).

Some papers showed evidence of counting words—little pencil marks in the margin—100 words, 200 words, 300 words, and finally, 495 words. (Nowadays computers count words.) Time to quit. After all, they had completed the assignment. I used to write a little "Hurrah!" or something similar beside the 495 or 500 to praise the writer.

Word-counting. We all do it. Should I have judged the student for barely making it to 500 words when I myself would probably be involved in the same game before long? Maybe not at the beginning of the school year when ideas and energy were fresh, or even the second month of instruction, but toward the beginning of May, when stacks of papers kept growing higher and higher, I knew I'd be asking, "How many words do I need to complete this year's teaching assignment?"

The word-counting stage in teaching began for me when I tallied the number of class periods, papers to grade, tests to make out, references to write, or committee meetings to attend. I knew word-counting had set in when my skin turned cold and clammy at the thought of English 102 handing in term papers—when some didn't even know where the *Reader's Guide to Periodical Index* was located in the library.

Word-counting set in with real force when several advisees during preregistration in late spring said, one after another, "I'd like to work with people" but refused to consider classes in interpersonal communications or anything to do with close interaction with other students. And I was word-counting with a vengeance when I decided not to check my mailbox, but instead hoped all memos, questionnaires, and other materials would self-destruct or turn moldy if I left them for a few days. I didn't want to make words, few or many, with anyone, at any time.

As a young mother, I was at the word-counting stage when I contemplated how many more years I would have to wash diapers and boil bottles daily, how many more noses to blow, how many more times to tell the children to hang up their clothes and to clean their rooms. As they grew older, word-counting evidenced itself in wondering how many more cans of hair spray and pairs of pantyhose I'd have to buy for the girls from a limited budget, how many more nights I would sit up waiting for someone to come home, how many more times I would have to urge the children to mow the lawn before someone pastured a cow on it.

Word-counting sets in for most of us as we get older. We know that time has come when there is no enthusiasm for another church committee meeting, even if it offers free scrambled eggs and bacon, pancakes with hot syrup, juice, hot cinnamon rolls with gooey icing, and coffee.

Word-counting can be a way of saying, "I'm lazy," but

often it's simply another way of saying, "I'm weary." Many frail elderly people arrive at that stage when they have lived longer than they intended to. Physical and psychic energy is depleted but the heart keeps pumping.

Whenever I phoned my mother in the last years of her life, her frequent comment was "Katie, I'm tired." She had lived more than her allotted three score years and ten and was ready to cross the border to a better land where all things become new, where her eyesight wouldn't fail her and her legs wouldn't give out. She was counting hours and days and wondering when she could stop living.

Walter Brueggeman has a significant chapter in his book *The Land* about the children of Israelite's border crossing into Canaan. Before Israel entered the Promised Land, there was a long reflective pause at the boundary as though the Israelites were reluctant to place their feet in the Jordan, dry though it would be. Israel knew the next steps would be a "walking away from the inscrutable nourishment of the wilderness."

The moment of the border crossing stands as a paradigm, writes Brueggeman, for what must occur at the boundary of a new land. The identity questions all have to be addressed again. The Israelites had to ask themselves who they were in relationship to Yahweh when the manna and the quail ceased and they had to provide their own food.

The land before them was a gift to Israel from Yahweh that bound Israel in new ways to the giver. But the land was also a source of temptation. The land invited Israel "to enter life apart from covenant" and to forget Yahweh and so cease to be an historical people, "open either to the Lord of history or to his blessings yet to be given."

Yet land to the Israelites was also a task. God entrusted

the land to the Israelites for them to share with all heirs of the covenant, "even those who have no power to claim it." The land also was a threat to the Israelites to settle for something short of what God wanted for Israel.

Gift. Temptation. Task. Threat.

All these elements are present in every border crossing, whether the person is a new immigrant to a country, a dependent elder like my mother waiting to cross over to the place where there is no death, or someone in Elder Stage Number One like myself, moving from retirement to new territory.

Mother and Dad and my two older sisters were new immigrants from Russia to Canada in 1923. They crossed the geographic border of the land of their birth to begin life anew in a strange country. The opportunity to migrate to a new land and make a new life was a gift from God. It was a gift of grace. Before them lay the land of Canada. Before them lay the task of making it their country. Mother and Dad always remained grateful for the opportunity, Dad silently, Mother openly.

Mother recently made another crossing. She told me that she was not afraid of the final border crossing before her. At nearly ninety-nine, she wasn't afraid to die, she said, or of being rejected by God. She and God had shared too much for God not to know her when she arrived at the gates of heaven. But she wondered with a kind of curiosity what it would be like on the other side and how wonderful it would be to see Dad again—and her parents. She had missed him—and them. But it was this time of waiting, when her life task had been completed, that was difficult. And she didn't know how many days or years to count before the end. She died in March 1994, two weeks before turning ninety-nine.

Marshall Jenkins in "Grandfather's Prayers" (*Christian Century*) writes that every time he visited his grandfather, the older man would ask for some clue that no mortal could give, some answer to the question, "Is my life worth living in this interim between my wife's death and mine? Is there anything I can do to get past this loneliness, this sense of worthlessness?" He was asking how many words he needed to fulfill his quota.

People are living longer and not knowing why. Society has gained from medical advances that allow people to live longer but has lost because the quality of life in old age has not improved. I believe the elderly have the right to ask, "Why can't I die?" when physical strength and meaningful experiences are at an end. We don't like to hear that. We want to deny them the right to say that, but it expresses a yearning to leave this life for a better one. I think they also have the right to mourn when they experience loss of any kind, whether meaningful existence, or a dream, a spouse, a home, or even a box of sentimental mementos of another era that couldn't come with them to the nursing home.

A robust Christian faith seems to demand that those who minister to the elderly cheer them up, said one gerontologist. And I was tempted sometimes to say to Mother, "Oh, you won't die for a long time yet," though I knew the dishonesty behind my words. What is a long time when you are nearly ninety-nine? And so I assured her of my love and prayed for a quick peaceful homegoing. God granted that request.

True Christian faith allows others to grieve, for Christ said, "Blessed are those who mourn," not "Blessed are those who refrain from mourning." Faith in Christ allows people to grieve, because the Lord understood sadness and aloneness, that it was part of his life. A stiff upper lip in time of sorrow may be good stoicism, but not good Christianity.

The apostle Paul was aware that God's children sometimes get weary, that they begin counting words, so he challenged the Corinthian church to "stand firm. Let nothing move you. Always give yourselves fully to the work of the Lord, because you know that your labor in the Lord is not in vain" (1 Cor. 15:58). Affirmation of older adults undergirds their faith with power. Denial or neglect of them takes away that strength. But for affirmation to happen, there needs to be a spiritual community or support group which values the older person.

An older woman shared with me that she was planning to move from her home, where she had lived forty years, to an apartment. The decision had been difficult yet necessary because of declining health. But the pain of letting go of her earthly belongings was cutting deep. Each week she filled the garbage bins with trash.

I gave her a hug. I was trying to understand. I had gone through a move two years ago and felt the same tug at my heart as I debated whether to keep something or throw it out. I could listen to her, affirm her, but she had to make the crossing to a smaller, more manageable place herself. Even more important, she had to move inwardly as well as physically and geographically. And moving the inner baggage is sometimes more difficult.

In ministering to the elderly, we are told, we should try to understand their hopes, dreams, ambitions, goals, depressions, and joys, for only "the old know what it means to be old." Their task is to arrive at integrity, to use Erik Erikson's term, to find out how it all fits together—not from the perspective of one caught up in the case, but as one who can see from a different perspective, from a greater distance. To understand them is to reenact the incarnation of Christ.

Jenkins answers his grandfather's question about what is life for when you are very old with another sobering statement, "If you [his grandfather] don't know after ninety-four years of sainted ministry what you can do in this interim between death and life to make yourself worthy of God's love, I don't know." His word to his grandparent was that all that was needed of him was to pray. Just keep praying. Nothing more important than that.

The grandfather kept

> "several dog-eared, yellowing books filled with names of missionaries, Bible translators, friends, and family members. Each day, for hour upon lonely hour, he leaf[ed] through these lists of names and pray[ed] for them—for missionaries he never met and for his own children and grandchildren.

In his prayers he brought the generations together.

Keep praying, Mother, I told her when she still alive. We need your prayers. We will miss them when you are gone. And I do already.

But what about those who like myself are also making a border crossing into uncharted country, as the Israelites did? Plutarch writes that early mapmakers added notes in the margins of their maps. The mapmakers stated that beyond the charted territory lay parts of the world they knew nothing about, except that they were filled with sandy deserts full of wild beasts and unapproachable bogs. Early geographers of Jonathan's Swift's time, for want of information about tribal communities, filled gaps in their maps of Africa with savage pictures of elephants.

One of our tasks as freshman elders is to make maps

for those coming after us, even as we check the maps of those who went before us, incomplete as they may be. We must fill in the uncharted regions of the new country of the aging, not with sandy deserts full of wild beasts or savage elephants and bogs, but with the hope of the gospel of Jesus Christ and the assurance that God is at work today, still reconciling and redeeming.

We must fill our maps of this new territory with stories of God's grace. We may be tempted to start with propositions and theological statements and theories of aging. All the way through this book I have been tempted to theorize about growing older and have had to discipline myself to look for the story instead.

Let's tell God's story. Let's tell the stories of God's people. Let's tell our stories. The Israelites were people on a journey, who glimpsed a city from afar, writes the apostle Paul. Here they had no continuing city. They expected God to deliver them and to bring them into the Promised Land. God did. And they told the story of the wilderness wandering and that God had always provided for their needs. The wilderness was a place of "enoughness," not of want. Maps need such stories of people who have found God to be faithful and true.

With the prophets, let's not entirely leave out warnings of the dangers and temptations of the road. Let's put up Caution, Danger, and Stop signs to show those coming after us that the enemies of the cross are much alive even as we grow older. Not all the exiled Jews in Babylon, when given their freedom, were eager to return to Judah. They had become accustomed to their captivity. Custom makes many practices endurable and comfortable, even if wrong.

Let's tell younger generations that sin is still sin, not just a careless goof. Unkindness always hurts. Harsh criticism always destroys. Prejudice always demeans. Violence, whether psychological or physical, violates the image of God in the person. Old age is the proving ground of whatever one has believed, taught, and said. It's now or never.

Let's fill our maps with dreams and bold visions, if not for our age group, then especially for the next generation. Let the visions be so bold we're uncomfortable explaining them. Eighty-year-old Caleb voiced a bold dream when he asked Joshua, the Israelite military leader of the conquest, to give him the mountain as his share of the territory. The strain of carrying out a vision is its strength. If there is no tension, there is no strength. A slack rope never pulled a stubborn cow out of the mud. You have to walk into the wind. You have to feel the strain. You have to cling to the neck of the eagle.

Let's fill our maps of the country ahead with opportunities for risk-taking for older adults. Lewis Carrol in the poem "The Hunting of the Snark" writes that one day the captain of the ship brought a large map to his men that showed only the sea, without the least vestige of land, and the crew "was much pleased when they found it to be a map they could all understand." They knew sea. They understood sea. It showed no unknown risks.

As we chart the unknown territory before us through experience, let's include challenges to those coming after us to take risks. Let's assure them the risk is always worthwhile. God has not promised success. They may experience pain. But if they fail, God's forgiveness is great enough to start again. We've traveled that way. We know.

Let's fill our maps of aging with the language of the poet and the celebrant as well as the professional. People long to hear the word that will be God's word to them. So let the words of the poet emerge. Let's not fear the language of symbol, of simile and metaphor, of condensed meaning, of truth couched in beauty. Such words may not provide any new fact or statistic. But they arouse the imagination, create the vision, and encourage the risk.

Let's show everyone that the pieces and parts of the territory we have traversed thus far fit together. Wendy's fast-food chain had an advertisement for their fried chicken in which a laidback employee of a rival firm assures a customer that "parts is parts"—nothing more. Our task as older adults in the faith community is to keep telling one another that parts are not just parts, but that the various members of the body of Christ form a unified whole. Included are men and women, old and young, all races and all social groupings. If we are not conscious of the other members of the body, we fall prey to the arrogance of believing that we are "splendidly solitary."

Yet having declared what our map will consist of, we need to remember that the map is not the territory, the word is not the thing, to use Hayakawa's well-known phrase. A map is an abstraction of reality. It is a pattern, an image, a picture, a plan. We bring meaning to maps as we do to pictures. Life is real.

The danger for mapmakers, young or old, is to want to take the journey, and even to make maps, without the expense, fatigue, and inconvenience of the heat, cold, hunger, and thirst of the journey. We would like to substitute Bible studies, workshops, sermons, conferences, and lectures for the journey itself and never get into the heat of the day. But the final years of the journey must be traveled, not in isolation but in community, as we tell our story, sharing our failures and conquests.

We young elders will find out that the maps we make

are never complete or completely accurate. Others will suggest better paths to move through the maze of aging than those we suggest. This doesn't matter. It is most important to be humble before God, faithful to the truths of God's word, and to trust in the primacy of grace. God is always greater than our ability to fully comprehend what his words to us are.

In early life our life journey seems clearly established. We follow the directions given to us by our parents and elders and act on their advice. Then suddenly we find ourselves at the head of the march. We are the Omegas, the last in the line. A sense of waylessness may overcome us. We encounter a struggle for integrity. We fear losing control, being shifted from center stage.

When Ezra led the first detachment of Babylonian exiles back to Zion, the Jews did not have the Shekinah glory the Israelites had when they wandered in the wilderness. When, as you move through the years, the track before you dies in the grass—and it will—and when the expanse of desert lies in front of you without a beaten pathway—and it also will—the task is to keep moving, to keep on the spiritual journey.

I found as I wrote this book that to embark on a spiritual journey of discovery placed me in a certain peril. I met fiery dragons and trumpeting elephants I didn't know existed in me. But I also found strength to continue when I recognized beasts of despair and doubt inside myself as well as in the jungles of the world and remembered that God commanded the journey into old age. If God has no plan for older adults, God really goofed. I was assured now he hadn't.

17

This gives me hope

What is faith? Faith is the eye by which we look to Jesus. A dim-sighted eye is still an eye; a weeping eye is still an eye. Faith is the hand with which we lay hold of Jesus. A trembling hand is still a hand. And [they are] believers whose hearts tremble within them when they touch the hem of the Savior's garment, that they may be healed.

Faith is the tongue by which we taste how good the Lord is. A feverish tongue is nevertheless a tongue. And even then we may believe, when we are without the smallest portion of comfort; for our faith is founded not upon feeling, but upon the promises of God.

Faith is the foot by which we go to Jesus. A lame foot is still a foot. The one who comes slowly, nevertheless comes.

—George Mueller (1805-1898)

Something was seriously wrong. I couldn't figure out what it was. I counted four days across my new datebook to write in an appointment, but instead of landing on Wednesday (the way all decent calendars are arranged), I landed on Thursday. Someone had obviously slipped a cog in designing my new datekeeper.

The days didn't match last year's book. In my new book, the first day of the week was Monday. Sunday was the last day of the week. Without apology. I turned to another new datebook. There it was again. Monday was the first day of the week, Sunday the last. Why?

For many working people, Saturday and Sunday come at the end of the week. They look forward to weekend discretionary time. For them, Monday, not Sunday, begins the new week. Calendars are simply adapting to this new way people think about the week.

Who uses Saturday today as a get-ready day for Sunday, the way families did a generation ago? In those days, potatoes had to be boiled to fry on Sunday to keep work to a minimum on that day. Clothes were brushed and pressed. Shoes were polished. Sunday school lessons were prepared. The BIG DAY was coming.

Today? People use Sunday to gear up for Monday—to wash the car, to mow the lawn, to do the laundry, and such stuff. The BIG DAY is Monday, when you either crawl or rush back into the harness of the weekly routine. Modern calendars reflect this new thinking.

Not only has our attitude toward the week changed, but also our concept of the length of a day. A poignant reminder of my childhood is the memory of my father promptly pulling the weights on our wall clock after the ten o'clock radio news. "Time for bed," he'd say and blow out a lamp or two. Because no one could read in darkness, we all headed up the stairs.

Today electricity extends the day into the night or even switches them around. Day and night have lost their natural boundaries through human invention and manipulation.

We also think about time itself differently. We manacle time to our wrists with terrifyingly complex timepieces to subdue time and all its components. We rivet it to our minds with a variety of program guides; schedules; and daily, weekly, monthly, and yearly planners. They're our defense against the drivenness of daily life. Through them we gain the whip hand over life. To be caught in circumstances not of our own choosing is to do time like a convict.

Unconsciously, I think, we also carefully schedule times for God to meet us—personal devotions, services, meetings. We tell God, "I'm here. Speak to me." If God fails to accept our invitation, that's God's problem; we're off to the next appointment. I doubt that we seriously expect God to interrupt us at committee and board meetings. In some tightly choreographed worship services, the Holy Spirit might have a hard time breaking in.

If we think differently about time, days, and weeks, we also think differently about the length of the years of our lives in this brave new world. Old Testament worshipers wanted to live a long life in order to have more years to be part of a worshiping community. The promise of long life appears often in wisdom sayings as a reward to those who fear God and keep his commandments.

I don't hear modern Christians agonizing in prayer for a long life, although some psychologists say we'd all have better mental health if we were eager to live to be a hundred. Instead I hear despair at the thought of living on and on and on, possibly with poor health, loneliness, and dependency. Suicide is not uncommon among old people, especially among older white males, for whom the waning of status and significant activity is a tremendous loss.

At the turn of the century, longevity was expected to

be about forty-seven years. Today it is closer to seventy-five for men and eighty-four for women, and the number of people over the age of eighty-five is steadily increasing. But the inner resources of these people are not always growing to meet the increasing years given them. For many older people, that accounts for the anxiety about the years ahead.

I flicked the page of the calendar to the new month to find a note to myself fluttering from underneath. "What gives you hope?" it read. Hope? I read the note again, not quite sure what I had intended when I first placed it beneath the calendar page. Was it a reminder to keep assuring myself that hope leads to grace, and that grace is available every day of the week and throughout life, not just during youth and middle age?

What gives me hope? I know much better what makes me hopeless.

When my computer screen flashes "Fatal Error," I know the time for hoping is over. Even prayer and weeping won't help. The matter is ended. I feel hopeless when a difficult situation I'm in has no immediate prospect of changing. The sisters Mary and Martha felt hopeless when Jesus delayed coming in response to their plea that their brother Lazarus was very ill. Hope trickles out like sand from a sieve when we think that God is nowhere within seeing, hearing, and touching distance—that Fatal Error is written over everything.

I took the challenge to answer the question. What gave me hope this week? Is the potential for grace as great when one is seventy or eighty as at sixteen or twenty-six? Can I draw a map of hope for those following me?

Southern writer Flannery O'Connor had tremendous insight into the working of God's grace. O'Connor calls the unexpected encounter with God the moment of grace. It's a transitional moment, perhaps at first of uneasiness. It's an unplanned moment, easily missed if one's attitude is "Sorry, but I don't do grace on Mondays." The older years are a time to take courage and to wait for breakthroughs of God's grace.

Several years ago I heard Rollo May explain that when the symbols and myths of a society are in full bloom, they absorb the people's anxiety and help them face change and death. When the symbols and myths die out, people become isolated and uncertain about their direction, for their symbols gathered them together.

To ridicule a culture's symbols or introduce a new one is a sure way to begin to break down that culture. In the 1950s the grey flannel suit, the symbolic uniform of the North American businessman, was ridiculed as the cookie-cutter symbol of the corporate world. When the black movement was gaining strength during the 1960s, the Afro hairstyle became a symbol of black unity. Likewise, young men who wanted to show their independence from their parents grew their hair long.

Rollo May gave an example from the Middle Ages. When people understood the religious symbols of the time, they lived without anxiety about death and life hereafter. When these symbols of a common faith disintegrated, the occult swept in. When the Greek myths, once powerful in holding the people together, lost their potency, there was room for the Judeo-Christian faith to be born.

What are the age-old symbols of old age that have given courage and strength to our society? Gray hair now stands for the frailty of body, yet it once stood for breadth of knowledge and experience and depth of wisdom and faithfulness. Older people were respected not for their age but for their accumulated wisdom and knowledge. In the church, they were acknowledged as those who had experienced the grace and goodness of God. This respect gave them a tranquil old age.

I sense our society lacks symbols representing the inner power and strength of old age. Organizations like American Association of Retired Persons stand for political and economic power, but not strength and generosity of spirit. And so we need to discover new symbols that will bring hope and grace and courage to this particular group.

I take hope when I see small signs (even bold gray hair) and vague symbols of aging emerging, with dignity and respect, even if slowly. I take hope as I watch people nurturing these signs and symbols.

I have often heard people relate their "best Christmas" or their "most disappointing" Christmas as part of a Christmas program. Digging through the store of memories can be valuable, even when alone, for through the backward journey we become familiar once again with the plot of our life story, the main characters, the conflict, and at which points in the action we allowed God's love and power to become part of the resolution. And especially, how we can make that power a part of the continuing pattern of life.

Like the patterns of Christmas, the patterns of life change over the years. Over the years, the plot of one's life story often moves in a direction never expected. I found that Christmas is possible without all family members, but not without people. Christmas is possible without gifts, although they do bring joy. Christmas is also possible without travel, programs, and banquets, but not without the assurance of love and that there will be strength to continue loving. And that is what Christmas is all about.

That is also what aging is all about. As one draws closer to the end-years, things (dolls with real hair and trains with motors), programs, and services, become less and less important. Continuing to experience breakthroughs of God's grace and mercy and to take courage for daily living become more important. Madeleine L'Engle writes in *The Irrational Season* that the nativity is "a time to take courage." What good did the infinite God coming in the form of a finite child do? she asks. Human beings are still evil.

I look about me. We still do not have the peace on earth of which the angels sang that first Christmas day. Words and armaments are piling up. Though the Bible is a best-seller, pornography is a close runner-up. Though interest in spirituality is increasing, families are still breaking up. Everywhere environmental resources are being depleted. People look, sometimes desperately, for answers to stress, tension, and change. Did Christ's coming change anything?

I take hope when I see older adults finding new and richer patterns for their lives and opening themselves to God's breakthroughs, even when it seems as if evil and violence are overcoming the world.

As I grow older, questions that concern me now are not the theological ones about eschatology, eternal security, and the unpardonable sin that excited me when I was a young Bible college student.

But I wonder about these: Why doesn't faith empower people to change more surely? Christian leaders are as guilty of sexual indiscretions as the main characters in a soap opera. Christian husbands abuse their wives. What has made the gospel anemic? Biblical promises don't carry fervent preacher-backed guarantees they once did of being divorce-proof, drug-proof, inflation-proof, and prejudice-proof. Even Christians suffer from these problems.

How can our society contain the force of evil and violence threatening our very lives? Why are affluent North American Christians reluctant to side with the poor?

Why do we make budgets that spend as much on sanctuary decorations as on meeting the needs of the poor?

I find Christian formulas don't seem to work as we were taught they would when we were young. Only if we stay isolated inside our closed church community, where life is still orderly and homogeneous, does the organized faith life make sense. To match the church's powers with the battle going on in the wider world of poverty, violence, suffering, oppression, and apathy seems like pushing a 6AAA shoe onto a 12EEE foot. So the motto on the wall, "Prayer changes things," is replaced in some homes by a still life of tropical fruit.

Yet people go through the religious motions they learned as young adults. They hope that the former zeal for truth and righteousness may yet return, that when the church gets another chance to speak out, it will be with power rather than cringing fear.

Christ came to share our living and our dying. The price of Christ's love was the pain of being human and of painfully giving up that life for us on the cross. He came to share my life. He came to share the joy of being human. He knows about it, for he is Emmanuel. Old age, like Christmas, is a time to move ahead with courage because God knows us in our humanity. Because of Christ's death, we can know him in his divinity. The message at this time of life is still Emmanuel—God with us.

I take hope when I see older adults steady in their faith even when the golden basket is empty, evil seems to have triumphed, and time seems to have stolen everything.

As I've mentioned, my parents came to Canada from Russia in 1923 and left behind many relatives. Those relatives in Russia always remained out of focus. That is, until one summer about fifteen years ago, when I met an aunt face-to-face, Mother's sister. She had migrated to Germany from the former Soviet Union and was visiting relatives in Canada. She had last seen my mother as a young girl of twelve. Now Tante Trude was sixty-nine.

Is an absence of nearly six decades enough to destroy family ties? Quite the contrary. My "new" Aunt Trude is short, slightly plumpish, like my mother. A strong family resemblance shows up in her facial features and red hair. I found it almost uncanny to meet for the first time a younger version of my mother. She talks, laughs, and gestures much the same way my mother did.

But family is more than flesh and blood. It is shared experiences of hope, joy, sorrow, and disappointment. I wanted to find out about the grandparents I had never known and the events of the missing years—from the time my parents left the Ukraine in 1923 with my two older sisters to the present.

What had the years of separation done to her? She told me about war, illness, death, famine, exile, hard work, prejudice, living as a refugee and as an exiled member of a work camp crew hauling stones, separation from loved ones, as well as stories of good times and happy events.

"What helped you the most?" I asked her in my Americanized German. My aunt is a quiet, withdrawing person, but she answered quickly and surely, *"Nur dem Halt am Herrn"* (Only by clinging to the Lord).

I sensed a simple faith, a steady faith, a Corrie-ten-Boom kind of faith, which endures despite difficult circumstances. I found Tante Truda remarkably free of bitterness toward any persons or any political body. Though life had been incredibly hard at times, almost beyond human endurance, she had chosen not to be governed by resentment.

Her story and stories like hers give me hope that God is a sovereign God, a God to be trusted, a God who gives grace to forgive and overcome.

A big computer was installed in the Pentagon. Of course, this was many decades ago. The computer was one of those early huge affairs with dials, wheels, lights, and so forth that filled a room. It could do just about anything—a real eighth wonder of the world—even translate Chinese into English and vice-versa.

A general was showing a senator around and asked, "Would you like to see it work?"

"Of course," said the senator.

"Well, type something into the computer and it will translate it into Chinese for you on the screen."

So he typed in the old saw, "Out of sight, out of mind."

In a matter of seconds, Chinese characters appeared on the screen, but no one could read Chinese to ascertain its accuracy. So they sent for someone fluent in Chinese. The young woman looked at the characters on the screen and reported, "It says, 'Invisible idiot.' "

Machines translate "Out of sight, out of mind" into "invisible idiot."

I take hope when I see people translate the pain and suffering of the human condition into the grace of God.

Without such stories of grace, our society will someday become a huge repository of computers and similar equipment, listing names and other significant data and translating words literally. But the glory of the Lord will have departed.

When Moses recited the stories of God's dealing with the Israelites, he was saying, "Here is the pattern for us—at the Exodus, in the wilderness, at the Jordan, when we received the Ten Commandments." It is a pattern of God's love and grace and hope.

I take hope when I am assured that hope is possible at all seasons of life.

> Though the fig tree does not bud
>> and there are no grapes on the vines,
> though the olive crop fails
>> and the fields produce no food,
> though there are no sheep in the pen
>> and no cattle in the stalls,
> yet I will rejoice in the Lord,
>> I will be joyful in God my Savior. Hab. 3:17-18

18

Border crossing

The yearning to belong somewhere, to have a home, to be in a safe place, is a deep and moving pursuit. —Walter Brueggeman

The thought came to me one morning, somewhat spontaneously, as I was driving, that I had crossed the border to the safe side of the land of the aging. The light had turned green. It was no longer amber. I was walking on solid ground, not the boggy turf on which I began this journey four or five years ago, and more specifically when I retired from teaching.

Once you cross a border, you look behind to see what kind of territory you have crossed. I could see the tracks I had been making, sometimes with slow steps, sometimes more quickly; sometimes stumbling, sometimes high-jumping.

I had dared to ask what it means to grow older. I had dared to confront my confusion, a confusion that had been grace. I had been willing to divest myself of illusions and false securities. The enemy no longer looked as fierce. I no longer felt trapped. New, bolder patterns were emerging out of the hesitancy with which I began my journey. I wanted to shout, Hallelujah.

With retirement I had been forced to join a minority that is becoming a growing majority yet is slipping to the edge of society. I had stood on that edge with these people and sensed the aggressiveness felt by some of the next generation; some chafe at the slowness with which today's older generation is dying. "Hurry up, hurry up!" they say, "You're taking too much time to die and spending too much of our money doing so."

I had felt their impatience with older adults who wouldn't relinquish positions of influence and power or who hampered the progress of businesses and institutions because they refused to master the new technology. I had felt the pain of those who wanted to contribute but were cast aside because their thinking was outdated.

I had heard with my own ears the voices of baby boomers denouncing the entitlement programs in which I was participating.

I had seen with my own eyes the increasing physical frailty of the older members of my age group by going into homes to serve as a hospice volunteer. I had seen the medical supplies and trays of medications beside bedsides and in bathrooms.

I had heard of the anger and impatience of nursing home workers with the weakness and ugliness of aging bodies that won't conform to expectations, sometimes resulting in abuse.

I had heard thoughtless language belittling the group I now was part of—and grasped even more its harsh meaning that these older adults were losing it and needed to step aside.

I had recognized the emphasis on individualism and

independence, often resulting in despair, futility, and loneliness. And I had been tempted to participate in the proffered activities (fun and games) that did not answer that emptiness.

In visiting with older adults, I knew firsthand that family bonding was sometimes nonexistent—a mere formality for some.

I had urged myself to be particularly careful about elder scams via telephone or door-to-door peddlers.

All of this spelled vulnerability. And weakness.

But that is only one side of it. What can older adults declare with the boldness of Martin Luther, who nailed his 95 theses to the door of the cathedral at Wittenburg?

Elijah had boldly proclaimed a drought for three years. Was he scared when he did so? Elisha had brought to life the Shunammite woman's son. Was he worried he was overstepping into God's territory? Jeremiah had announced with much weeping the destruction of Jerusalem and Isaiah the promise of the Israelite's return from exile.

The story is told that at a baseball game a little boy watched a male television star. Other kids were getting autographs, but he found it wonderful just to stand and look at his idol. Finally he approached the man and stared some more. And some more. At last he said with awe to the idol, "Do you know who you are?"

How long has it been since the church has asked the older adult, "Do you know who you are?" Probably too long, because the reply one often gets is, "Yeah, sure. I know who I am. I'm getting old. My face is wrinkled, my hair is thin, my bones ache, my get-up-and-go has got up and gone. Sometimes I feel sort of useless, often lonesome. I know who I am—just a tired old discard."

So I say to myself, to all older adults, "Old man, old

woman, do you know who you are? What are you saying with boldness?" Some of us just over the border are trying to figure this out. And this is my one answer: This can be a grace-filled stage of life.

I used to teach a college course in Old Testament literature. In our study of the lament form of the psalms, we noted how the psalmist frequently looked back to identify for himself God's working in his life and that of Israel in the Red Sea delivery, the careful provision for sustenance in the wilderness, the support during the conquest. In writing their own psalms, what could young college students point to in the past? That was a tough assignment for them —to look back and see God's grace and mercy. It was easy to see what money can do for a family. It buys houses, cars, boats, electronic equipment, CDs, vacations. But what has God done for them as individuals, families, and congregations? Some drew blanks.

In the first year of retirement, I listened to three groups of older adults discuss the same question: Where is the evidence of God's grace and power working in your life?

Several types of answers that dominated the discussion troubled me. If the event seems miraculous and probably won't be explained by science, for example, a healing that shouldn't have taken place according to the doctor's prognosis, it is of God.

If the event involves coincidence, it is of God. For example, if you needed money and found $500 while jogging, God was with you. Likewise, if at the intersection the car plowing through a red light barely misses yours. Or if a tornado destroys a neighboring town but your community is spared. Or if the hailstorm destroys the fields in the area, but your flower garden stands straight and beautiful. All are evidence of God working on your behalf.

The same holds true if something you have prayed about ends up for your good. Your favorite team wins. You are out of a job and get one at once. I read a Sunday school story paper in which a father and son were flying a kite out in the field, when a sudden gust of wind tore it out of the boy's hands and it soared skyward. Father and son prayed for the return of the kite; it came back.

By implication, God is asleep at the wheel when the accident does happen, a person does not get well, the storm hits your home, the kite does not return. Some of the answers I was hearing seemed to say that God is at work when anything occurs that can't be explained by resorting to natural or behavioral sciences, yet needs an explanation. The gap is attributed to God. "Lord, I can see your hand in this," we say, especially if it is a single dramatic event.

People long for miracles, for big spiritual experiences, not just the little emotional ripple we sometimes experience during worship. We want God to reveal himself to us. We want a conscious experience of God. We want experiences we can testify about, write a book about, maybe even that will make us rich and famous. And I'll admit that while writing this book at times I longed for the big powerful revelation from God. Then I would have had fascinating miracles to write about in masterful language, instead of my plucking word after word out of my mind, deleting, and trying again. I think that some people in those discussions were trying to find that big revelation of God in their past as we discussed God's miracle-working power.

I don't deny God's power and providence in crisis events. God deals with us in crises in special ways. Yet missiologist Paul Hiebert states that when we focus on the dramatic, the unusual, as evidence of God's working, we secularize our lives. We set up two categories: the sacred and the secular. The sacred is anything that seems miraculous; the secular is everything else. If we can explain the event by science, it is secular. If we can't explain it, it is supernatural—and God gets the credit. We push God into a smaller and smaller corner with such thinking, allowing him to work only in certain areas of our lives.

Popular religious books and articles today are about big spectacular events—recovery from drug addiction, release from crime, miraculous healing from cancer, dramatic escapes from death. In John 14:7, the disciple Philip asks Jesus, "Show us the Father." Jesus replies, and I think there is sorrow in his voice, "Have I been so long time with you, and yet have you not known me, Philip?"

Today Jesus would make the same statement to young and old. "Open your eyes and notice that I am with you. See those people who have transcended themselves to love others." God's miracles happen all the time—only they aren't accompanied by a display of neon lights or the blare of loudspeakers.

I participated in another discussion. Here people mentioned miracles also, but not the big healing with tumors disappearing or people being brought from the near dead. The focus was on the steady working of the Spirit to produce holiness, or Christ-likeness.

I went home to think through what I had heard. God is working in people's lives. No doubt about that. I could come up with example after example of the slow working of the Spirit of Christ. When we identify this often undramatic working of God in people's lives, making them more like Christ, we have located the spokes in the wheel of faith.

I made a fast sweep of people I knew.

A retired couple spent the summer constructing houses for the poor with Habitat for Humanity. That was grace.

An older couple was searching for help with a difficult family problem and was determined not to give way to despair and separation. That took grace.

A retired man spent several weeks with a medical surgeon in a West Africa mission as a fix-it man. He came back all fired up to do more—and went back at his own expense. Again, evidence of grace.

An older woman told me she spent her spare time telephoning lonely people regularly.

My elderly mother mentioned the care group from church who visited her in her apartment to sing and fellowship over refreshments following the death of my father. They were a visit from the Christ to her.

Another older woman, about eighty-five, told me of the good thing that had happened to her on Saturday. The youth group had washed all the windows and storm windows on her house and her neighbor's. A retired friend was coming to help her clean once a week.

An older woman, without children, has become the volunteer "grandmother" of several young couples with children.

These stories, like the inner assurance that I was traveling in safe territory, are as real as breakfast pancakes and sausage. So is a new understanding of a biblical truth and the courage to live it out. You've read something ten, maybe twenty times, worried about something a hundred times more. Then suddenly the murkiness clears and you can see clearly. Words that were just sound bites became meaningful truth.

You knew all along about forgiveness, about caring for the weaker person, about the need to affirm others, but that kind of knowledge is public. Then strangely, in a sermon, a book, a poem, the enlightenment of the Spirit broke through and you could say, "Aha! I have learned something new. This truth territory now belongs to me. I claim it for myself. Something new has begun in me."

That's the way I felt about my new thoughts about myself. I could say boldly that *old* is not a four-letter word. Old is a time of growth and grace. Old means triumph of hope over frustration and failure. I recall the time I first got to the end of the piano piece as a child at the same time as the metronome and how good it felt. Now the task is to get to the end of life and keep trusting.

I remember the first time I fixed a garbage disposal, made a computer obey my commands, watched my daughter walk for the first time after a long illness, listened joyfully to the stumbling words of unfamiliar faith from an adult. "Amen," I said then. "Amen," I say now, for I can put the words of Scripture into the past tense: God has revealed his love to me. Grace has been sufficient.

I feel released to listen to the voice of God calling me to reach even as Paul writes to the Philippians, to press onward "with arms outstretched." Convictions about many matters had been lying scattered in the corridors of my mind, struggling for recognition and resolution these three or four years. Now the freedom has come to work with them again. I can shout, "Aha!" joyously.

But I don't want to forget the "Huh?" experiences. I don't want to deny or forget every hurdle of discomfort, every doubt, every question about aging. When I stop walking around an idea to see the other side, when I stop asking questions of those who have encountered what I am going through, when I stop probing the depths of my beliefs for soundness, my inner life shrivels.

One evening as I looked over a large union service, I

noticed a predominance of snowy heads. Sitting there contemplating their faithfulness in church attendance, in giving, in praying, and in other types of service, I wondered whether the time hasn't come to respect anew the wisdom, stability, and insight of older adults. These were people whose wisdom surpasses textbook manuals, whose loyalty and faithfulness to Christ and the church and to spouses seldom wavers, whose generosity of time, energy, and money remains constant.

Each age has its own temptations. I do not belittle the temptations of the older population. These are frequently difficult for a younger mobile person to understand. How can one put oneself into the worn slippers of an eighty-year-old who feels forsaken because of fewer visits, fewer letters, and who has less physical and emotional strength with which to cope? The denial of a car license because of poor eyesight becomes a major catastrophe. The decision to move into a nursing home or retirement center seems equal to signing a major surrender treaty. Always there is the feeling of being managed, of being moved to the siding like an empty traincar.

The encouraging sign to me was that I had had courage to think through and reshape my theology of aging, to sort out cultural accretions regarding aging from beliefs. And to have done this kind of sorting, particularly in times of dryness, emptiness, and foggy vision, has meant greater certitude—and greater recommitment. I have tried to let go of what I could not hang onto, to recognize the larger patterns of growth possible for me at this time of life, to envision new possibilities, and to move on. The act of untangling and rebraiding brought clarity to my thinking.

And so I end this book by beginning to formulate a creed for the older adult.

1. God is. (Only two words, but here I begin.)

2. God loves me as I am—skinny, fat, wrinkled, bald, gray-haired, stooped over, erect. God loves me in every living arrangement—my own home, an apartment, nursing home, or retirement center. Nothing can separate me from God's love, neither life nor death, pain nor joy, divorce nor marriage, my fears nor my boasts, my arthritis nor my agility, other's prejudice toward the elderly nor their indifference. Nothing.

3. Jesus Christ, our Redeemer, is God in human form. He knows our temptations to become discouraged, lonely, and frustrated when weakened hands can't open a can of soup or dimming eyes can't read the newspaper or the Bible.

4. Human sin is a reality for all ages. Older adults are tempted to become angry and bitter, to harbor jealousy and exhibit discrimination, to carry grudges developed in middle age with great delight into their waning years, to refuse to change. Yet God's forgiveness through Christ and the courage to change is also a reality.

5. The Bible is the Word of God, yet I and everyone else who interprets it is fallible. I have to keep trying to learn how God's revelation in that Word is significant to me. And I pray for grace to let go of unfounded interpretations that were part of the religious culture of my youth and of interpretations today which make discipleship less costly.

6. Through faith in Christ, I am joined to other members of his body. To be a Christian in isolation is incongruous. The body exists to witness the power of the resurrection of Jesus Christ. As someone has said, the "sort of life required of Christians is too difficult and peculiar to survive without the church." We need a strong church to

stand against the darkness of this world.

But the church may not always remember who and where I am as I grow older. And that pain will surface. I echo what Elizabeth Welch says in *Learning to Be 85,* "It would be difficult for me to reach eighty-five believing that God loves me, if all the way God's world has rejected me."

Movies sometimes illustrate truths of the Christian life with keen perspecuity. In the film *Cool-Hand Luke,* the main character, an inmate in a correctional institute, has been through a siege of harassment by his overseers, including severe physical punishment and a period of isolation in the "box" in an attempt to break him. He is sick and unable to eat. But the director warns him that, unless he finishes his heaping plate of food, he faces another four days in the box, which is certain to end his life.

His fellow inmates watch him struggle with the food. Then slowly, one by one, they each pass him, grabbing a spoonful of his food to save him from further pain. That brief scene is a powerful image of community. I pray that there will be someone around to help me eat whatever life has dished up for me when I feel boxed in.

7. Faith without works is dead. Yes, dead. The Christian message of salvation is both a gift and a task. It cannot be possessed unless shared with others. But what are works when life is limited to a narrow bed in a small room? The work of faith then becomes *being.* Any person is always more than the sum of what he or she does.

8. The power of the Spirit enables a person to grow and to change. I want to keep believing that God gives grace in crisis and strength for the impossible. As a young adult, the youth group of which I was a member had sent me on to Bible college with the verse, "He which hath be-

gun a good work in you will perform it until the day of Jesus Christ." I left that small group with the firm conviction God would work in and through my life. And God kept that promise. But does that promise only hold until I reach the magic figure of sixty-five? Of course not.

9. Christian action does not guarantee that good will always triumph. Yet God can bring good out of any situation. And we have to keep fighting sin and evil.

10. There is life after death, a victory for faith, and defeat for death.

I enjoyed teaching James Baldwin's short story, "Sonny's Blues," in college literature classes. The younger brother, Sonny, a blues piano player, struggles with deciding between the temptations of the slums of Harlem and the white ambitions of his older brother. Harlem offers him heroin, which makes him feel in control. But Harlem also gives him the experience of jazz, which sets him free. The religious institutions of Harlem have done little to help his suffering.

Then one night, at a night club, the black bass violinist, Creole, and the other band musicians begin to play. Creole urges Sonny to play. "He wanted Sonny to leave the shore line and strike out for the deep water. He was Sonny's witness *that deep water and drowning were not the same thing*" (italics mine). And Sonny responds and plays jazz as he has never played before. He learns he does not have to reject Harlem to find his soul.

The land of aging may look like deep water. It did to me at first. But like Sonny, I am learning that deep water and drowning are not the same thing. The water may get deeper, and I think it will. But I want to remember that going in beyond my depth means trusting more.

Bibliography

Brueggeman, Walter. *The Land: Place as Gift, Promise, and Challenge in Biblical Faith.* Philadelphia: Fortress, 1977.

Butler, Robert N. *Why Survive? Being Old in America.* New York: Harper, 1975.

Comfort, Alex. *A Good Age.* New York: Simon & Schuster, 1976.

Davies, Robertson. "The Writer's Conscience," *Saturday Review,* March 18, 1975.

Dillard, Annie. *Teaching a Stone to Talk: Expeditions and Encounters.* New York: Harper & Row, 1982.

Dudley, Carl S. and Melvin E. Schoonover. "After the Hurricane," *Christian Century,* June 2-9, 1993

Elull, Jacques. *Living Faith: Belief and Doubt in a Perilous World.* San Francisco: Harper & Row, 1983.

Erikson, Erik, Joan M. Erikson, and Helen Q. Kivnick. *Vital Involvement in Old Age: The Experience of Old Age in Our Time.* New York: Norton, 1986.

Friedan, Betty. *Fountain of Age.* New York: Simon & Schuster, 1993.

Hammarskjold, Dag. *Markings.* New York: Knopf, 1964.

Jenkins, Marshall. "Grandfather's Prayers,"*Christian Century,* March 10, 1993.

Maitland, David J. *Looking Both Ways: A Theology for Mid-Life.* Atlanta: John Knox, 1985.

McNeil, John A. B. "On Becoming a Ulyssean," *The Ulyssean Adult.*

Overstreet, Harry. *The Mature Mind.* New York: W. W. Norton, 1949.

Proghoff, Ira. *At a Journal Workshop: The Basic Text and Guide for Using the Intensive Journal Process.* New York: Dialogue House Library, 1975.

Simundsen, Daniel J. *Hope for All Seasons: Biblical Expressions of Confidence in the Promises of God.* Minneapolis: Augsburg, 1988.

Steenland, Sally. "Prime Time Woman: An Analysis of Women on Entertainment TV," *Media & Values,* Winter 1989, No. 45.

Tiessen, Hildegard E., ed. *Forever Summer, Forever Sunday: Peter Gerhard Rempel's Photographs of Mennonites in Russia, 1890-1917.* St. Jacob's Ont.: Sand Hills Books, 1981.

Tournier, Paul. *The Seasons of Life.* Richmond, Va.: John Knox, 1960.

Welch, Elizabeth. *Learning to Be 85.* Nashville: Upper Room, 1991.

Whitehead, Evelyn Eaton and James D. Whitehead. *Christian Life Patterns: the Psychological Challenges and Religious Invitations of Adult Life.* Garden City, New York: Doubleday, 1979.

Wiebe, Katie Funk. *Life After Fifty: A Positive Look at Aging in the Faith Community.* Newton, Kan.: Faith & Life, 1993.

Wiebe, Katie Funk. *Prayers of an Omega: Facing the Transitions of Aging.* Scottdale, Pa.: Herald Press, 1994.

Fiction

Baldwin, James. "Sonny's Blues." *Dark Symphony: Negro Literature in America,* James A. Emanuel and Theodore L. Gross, eds. New York: The Free Press, 1968.

Masquez, Gabriel Garcia. *One Hundred Years of Solitude.* Harper, 1970.

Paton, Alan. *Cry, the Beloved Country.* New York: Charles Scribner's Sons, 1948.

Salinger, J. D. *Catcher in the Rye.* New York: Little, Brown, 1951.

Schaffer, Peter. *Equus.* Atheneum Publishers and Andre Deutsch, Ltd., 1974.

Steinbech, John. *East of Eden.* New York, Penguin, 1952.

Solzhenitsyn, Alexander. *One Day in the Life of Ivan Denisovitch.* New York: Bantam, 1963.

The Author

Katie Funk Wiebe, professor emeritus of Tabor College (Kan.), retired in 1990 after twenty-four years of teaching English at Tabor. She attended the Mennonite Brethren Bible College for two years and is a graduate of Tabor College (B.A.) and Wichita State University (M.A.). She is now working as a free-lance writer and editor.

In addition to hundreds of articles, Wiebe has written or edited thirteen books. These include such additional-Herald Press books as her 1994 *Prayers of an Omega: Facing the Transitions of Aging, Bless Me Too, My Father, Good Times with Old Times: How to Write Your Memoirs.* She has also written *Life After Fifty: A Positive Look at Aging in the Faith Community; Alone: A Search for Joy.* Wiebe was a columnist for *The Christian Leader* for thirty years. She has written four *Adult Bible Study Guides.* She was editor of *Rejoice!* (an inter-Mennonite devotional guide) for nearly five years. She continues as a workshop and retreat leader on topics primarily related to the older adult.

Wiebe grew up in northern Saskatchewan, the daughter of Russian Mennonite immigrants. In the Funk home, storytelling was part of the family tradition. She moved to Kansas in 1962.

She has traveled to India, Bangladesh, Nepal, the Soviet Union, Europe, and most recently to Central America with a Mennonite Central Committee learning group.

Wiebe is a member of the Mennonite Brethren Board of Resource Ministries, the Peace Education Task Commission of the United States Mennonite Brethren Conference, and a member of the board of the Center for Mennonite Brethren Studies in Hillsboro. Wiebe attends the First Mennonite Brethren Church in Wichita, Kansas, where she now lives. She has four children and five grandchildren.